From Mayhem To Miracles

Experiencing the powerful presence of God through the tragedy of the death of a child.

Mark R. Triplett

Adamstar Publishing

From Mayhem To Miracles

By Mark Triplett

Cover by Lydia Steward Design

Photos by
Mark Triplett Photography, LLC

All scripture references are from the
Holy Bible - New International Version

Printed in the United States of America

Bayport Printing House, Inc.
102 Central Avenue, Bayport, MN 55003

First Edition

Adamstar Publishing, LLC
www.adamstar-publishing.com

ISBN 978-0-9839603-1-7

To My Son

Adam

Contents

Foreword by Dr. Lisanne D'Andrea-Winslow   vi

Acknowledgements   xiii

Introduction   xx

Three Miracles of God's Love   1

1. Adam – My Son   3

2. Mark – Adam's Dad   29

3. Mayhem – The Thief   49

4. My Grief – The Villain   77

5. Miracles – Evidence of God's Love   99

6. Meaning – Unlocking The Mystery   157

7. Friends - A word from Adam's Mom   167

Foreword

"Aim For The Heart"

The book you are holding in your hand right now is a precious story, a powerful piece of writing that will change the way you experience grief and loss. I knew this even before I read a single word of the manuscript. It was through the story that you are about to enter, that my life, and my own grief journey, was directed toward healing, growth, and most importantly, toward trusting the Almighty God.

Mark and Linda Triplett entered my life at one of the most devastating periods of my life. After having just lost my husband, I was facing widowhood at the age of 46 with two young daughters to raise alone. Mark came to my home to help with some house projects that I was unable to do on my own. He was part of our church ministry, "Servants on Call." It was at our first meeting, as Mark with hammer in hand, told me how he and his wife Linda had lost a twenty-three year old son more than a decade ago. Their son was named Adam.

I listened intently to their story. Every word Mark revealed about the devastating loss of their son, about his wrangling with God and his faith, penetrated my broken heart and resonated with every fiber of my being. I, too, lost a son a decade ago and now with my infant son and my husband in side-by-side graves, Mark's words became a soothing balm to the ragged wreckage of my heart. I could deeply relate to his expression of utter despair over Adam's sudden tragic death in a plane crash.

I connected with the pervading spiritual struggle he experienced in the days and weeks after Adam's death. Struggles of thinking he was being punished by God, or that he somehow caused Adam's death. In my own grief and confusion, I had experienced many of these same struggles. I realized that although all of our stories of loss and grief are unique and very individual, we, as Anne Weems so eloquently puts it, *"Those who weep, and those who weep with those who weep"* are deeply connected to a life experience that can only be understood by the sad, tragic living of it.

Mark told me how thirteen years ago he wrote a book about Adam's death, a book that included his deep grief, wrestling with guilt and shame, confusion and blame. He told me how he processed his way through the muddy waters of these questions, much like the fictional character, Christian, in *A Pilgrim's Progress* plows through the Slough of Despond. This was pure *mayhem*. Mark's daily walk was in the chaotic disorder of sadness, confusion, loss, guilt and fear; it was the resounding chaos of grief. Yet, in spite of the mayhem, Mark set his mind, heart, and spirit on seeking God for answers to the deep, pervading questions of his heart. And, yes, the answers came.

The comfort, the beauty, the strength of God's abiding presence came to Mark in a variety of forms. We call them *miracles*. The miracles came in ways that neither you nor I could have ordained or predicted. But God, knowing Mark and Linda's hearts, spoke to them in a language that they knew and understood. A strange "smudge" that appeared on a web page they created for Adam; a smudge that took the shape of a heart and appeared on Linda's birthday, only on their computer. Messages came in the form of car license plates, from airplanes flying overhead, or from the loss of a treasured pen that mysteriously brought a message of hope. Mark was "tuned in" to the miracles that were happening all around him.

I knew, after hearing this incredible story of God's restorative power after the death of a child that I simply had to read Mark's manuscript. I felt a strong message from the Lord telling me to use my expertise in scholarly writing, editing and publishing to edit this manuscript, that Mark needed my help with getting his book in print, as much as I needed his help with putting up mini blinds and fixing the broken fence in my yard. Little did I know, nor could I have imagined then, how God would knit our hearts together in a deep, caring friendship where we walk alongside one another, in our brokenness, on this lifelong path of grief and recovery. Yes, this was yet another of God's miracles in our midst.

As we began the editing process, I came to know Adam through the eyes of his father. I learned how at age five Adam fell in love with flight and set out on a lifelong pursuit of becoming a pilot. I learned of his passion for music and his accomplishments as a gifted trumpet player. I read in awe of how he left his family and friends to pursue ministry training at the Moody Bible Institute in Chicago.

I began to form a relationship with this young man, now 13 years in Heaven, who I wept over never having had the opportunity to meet. I felt cheated, being robbed of the chance to know him on this earth. I felt that *humanity* was cheated, being robbed of having Adam Triplett, "Trippy" as his loved ones called him, on this earth to live out the full expression of who he was over the course of a lifetime.

How can one not look heavenward and ask, in all reverence and humility.... "Seriously now Lord...why, WHY take this gifted, talented, twenty-three year old passionate man, who loved You and served You with all of his heart, soul, mind and strength??? WHY???" I, with eyes of faith, know that God's ways are so far above ours and His thoughts so high above ours. He, in His wisdom knows how He has used and will use Adam and his story on this earth in ways that we may never know this side of eternity. But, oh, what a mystery it is.

I was so deeply moved when Mark and Linda gave to me a CD that they made to distribute to friends and loved ones after Adam's funeral. On this precious recording were several trumpet pieces that Adam played at orchestral concerts as well as a sermon that Adam delivered at Wildwood Church on September 3rd, 1995. I was moved to tears hearing Adam's voice. I felt as if I was in that church service hearing him proclaim God's message of love, forgiveness and hope.

Hearing Adam's voice on that recording made Adam *real* to me. It became more than learning of a sad and tragic story about a family who lost a son; I connected with Adam Triplett, *the person*. His words and the sound of his voice penetrated my heart and I grieved the loss of this amazing young man. As I listened to Adam play the piece *Aim for the Heart,* a composition by Billy Armstrong, written for Doc Severinsen of the Tonight Show Orchestra, I realized how that title captured the essence of Adam's life.

The story of his death will aim directly for your heart, as will the journey of his parents in finding the necessary meaning revealed in the message of hope and healing that only God's love can bring. This story will indeed aim for your heart. You are reading this book because you suffer in your own process of grief, or you know of someone who has.

The story of Adam Triplett's life is one that I trust will open your heart. His father, Mark, in this tender, embracing story will lead you down one family's path of sorrow and loss, choosing *all along the way* to seek God's purpose and plan; to rely on the "love that never fails" as Adam so beautifully declared in his sermon at Wildwood Church just two years before he entered God's holy presence.

It has been an honor for me to work with Mark on this book. I feel that I have received from Mark and his honest, poignant writing far more than I have given in the form of grammatical and structural suggestions. I have begun to seek God for the miracles in my own spiritual processing of the loss of my son and my husband.

I have received deep inner healing resonating with the questions Mark expounds, feeling less alone in the private world of my own grief. It is my hope that, after reading Mark's story of mayhem, and how God has turned that mayhem into miracles, you will be encouraged in your understanding and processing of grief and loss. I pray that you, too, will seek to turn mayhem into miracles in your own life. *Peace.*

Dr. Lisanne D'Andrea-Winslow
Professor of Biology
Northwestern College
St. Paul, MN

Acknowledgements

When writing this book, reflecting on all those who aided me in my journey in life, and ultimately through this dark *valley of grief*, I held to one precept, that through it all the miracle of love was always there.

Love was there in the life of Linda, Adam's mom, in the birthing room when Adam was born, and in the agonizing months after his birth dealing with colic and a strong will. Love was there when she made after school treats, and discussed the details of his day. Love was there when she calmed him and gave reassurance in the night during a thunderstorm or when he was sick. Love was there as she attended every music recital, every scout meeting, every soccer game, his high school graduation ceremony, his wedding, and ultimately his funeral. I thank you Linda, for your commitment to being the love that was always there, consistently throughout Adam's life.

Love was there in the presence of friends and family who fed us and prayed for us while we strained to deal with the greatest loss imaginable. I thank God for brothers, sisters, parents, cousins, aunts and uncles, some of whom traveled across the country to be by our side. Church family, like Dr.

Ron Johannson who not only ministered to our broken hearts but provided medical assistance and direction.

Love was there when neighbors Cindy Markfort and Mary Smith rallied the entire neighborhood to place over a thousand luminary candles lining both sides of our street representing an airport runway for Adam to *find his way home to us* in the night after the accident. I thank God for loving neighbors.

Love was there when all the flight instructors of Wings, Inc. of St. Paul, Minnesota flew the Missing Man Formation overhead at the funeral in honor of a fallen pilot and friend, moving the crowd to tears. I thank God for the loving co-workers and employer of Adam.

Love was there when Norm Schweitz, a church family member and fellow pilot donated a memorial plaque for Adam on the Aviator's Memorial Wall at the Wittman Regional Airport in Oshkosh, Wisconsin. Thank you Norm, for being a true friend to us and to Adam, and for your support of his flight training. We cherish your gift beyond words. God bless you!

Love was there in the gentle care of Dr. Marcus Bachmann, our therapist and true Christian friend, who helped us both see the light of reason and hope in a world filled with confusion and despair. Thank you Dr. Bachmann!

Love was there in my darkest hour, when I struggled with my own personal sin and guilt in the aftermath of Adam's death, through Christian leaders like Joyce Meyer, Dr. Billy Graham, and Dr. James Dobson, who all, through their fine staff members, counseled me in God's Word, giving me hope and reassurance.

The miracle of love was most certainly there when Dr. Ravi Zacharias personally spent time with me on the phone from his Georgia office and later met with me in Minnesota. I am honored that he added the story of Adam's death and my struggles in his book *Jesus Among Other Gods*. God bless you Dr. Ravi!

Love was most definitely there in the generous financial gift by Bill and Millie Messerschmidt, urging us to start a memorial scholarship fund in memory of Adam. That generous gift, and more that followed, allowed us to create *LNF Ministries*, the non-profit organization that oversees *The Adam M. Triplett Memorial Scholarship Funds*, and our *Love Baskets* ministry that provide families grieving the death of a child with hope, guidance and loving support.

William "Bill" Messerschmidt became a friend of our family through a professional connection with Adam and his music. Bill is a musician of the finest stock, a classical pianist and famed organist in Minnesota, Wisconsin and internationally. Adam was blessed to join the company of Bill Messerschmidt and have him as mentor, musical guide and friend. Bill is an experienced choral director and piano teacher. His skill and passion with the pipe organ is unmatched. Bill has played such notable pipe organs as the one in the Notre Dame cathedral in Paris, France.

Bill became a true friend to Adam and later a most cherished friend of Linda and me. It was Bill and Millie who presented us with a one thousand dollar check with instructions to *"...use this to start a memorial scholarship fund."* We did and today Bill is still on our Board of Trustees of LNF Ministries, our non-profit organization that serves two scholarship funds and our love basket grief support ministry.

Within the first few weeks after the death of Adam, we received a copy of an article that ran in New Richmond News, a small local newspaper in New Richmond, WI. It was about Adam, and Bill's experience with our son's life and legacy. Bill and Millie not only blessed us with money to start the scholarship funds, but also blessed us with announcing to the world, especially the town's folk of New Richmond, WI the beauty of our son's life and his legacy that lives on today. Following is that article in Bill's own words.

~~~~~~~~~~~~

Letters to the Editor
Crash victim was newlywed, fine man

To the Editor:
 A fiery tragedy touched your community on Aug. 4, a plane crash which took the lives of two young men. I join all who wish to express our sympathies to their families.

 I was most fortunate to have come to know one of the victims, Adam Triplett, the pilot-instructor. And I know I speak for so many others when I say that Adam touched our lives in some very special ways. It was truly an honor I shall always cherish, and I wanted you to know a bit about him.

 Most importantly, Adam lived a life of integrity and had a rock-solid Christian faith. He and his sister were brought up that way by loving parents. In 1992, I met Adam when he and a friend played trumpet for the church where I served as organist. Immediately I sensed his caring, helpful, unassuming ways.

 Later, he shared with me his dream of someday serving in aviation mission ministry, perhaps in Africa.

Although this was put on hold, he continued flight training, served the youth in his church, and played his trumpet superbly. Only recently did I find out he had been voted the number one trumpeter in Minnesota as a high schooler.

We will miss this young man, very much. Tragically he left behind his wife of only [three] months. I shared some of this with Scott Peirson when I stopped by to see the crash site. But I wanted to tell you too, because if ever there was a young person, so well developed personally and spiritually, it was Adam. I would hope my 5-year-old daughter could one day have the chance to be encouraged on in life by a young adult of his caliber. Many, many people feel the same way. The two-mile long cortege of vehicles out to Lake Elmo Airport for a special aviation tribute after the funeral was a testament to this. And now, with one scholarship program already established in his memory, by Wings Inc. and another memorial scholarship being considered, for the music or mission field, the legacy of this fine person lives on. He will most definitely be missed, but he surely won't be forgotten.

William Messerschmidt
St. Paul, MN

Bill and Millie have since moved from the Twin Cities to serve the Lutheran Church community of Mosinee, Wisconsin. We continue to keep Bill on our Board of Trustees and always will. His daughter has grown to be a fine young woman. Adam would have called her "friend". We consider it a miracle of the love of God to have Bill, Millie and Kristin in our lives.

Love was always there, no matter what the circumstance. It has no boundaries, no limitations, and no breaking point. Love has strength and a tenderness that defies human definition and understanding. Love finds a way when there is no way. Love is faithful and true. Love truly cares. Love never fails.

"God is Love."
1 John 4: 16 NIV

Introduction

When I began writing this book in 1998, I titled it *Love Never Fails*, attempting to bring some hope into the broken hearts of parents who have experienced the death of a child. I wanted to assure my readers that God's love will always be there, and will never fail them. However, reflecting on my own experience with loss and suffering, I quickly realized THAT is about the last thing a grieving parent wants to hear. Love doesn't seem to be evident at that most horrific time of their lives. Love doesn't seem to be present at all. It seemed like love failed, at least on that score.

Grieving parents feel deeply lost in their sorrow and helpless in the brokenness of their lives. There is absolutely no reasoning to this thing called death, especially the death of a precious child. Children are not supposed to die before their parents. Children are supposed to live long, prosperous lives! Death brings mayhem, destruction, disorder and pain. Where in all of that can anyone find love?

Looking back on the battlefield of my own sorrow and loss, in the aftermath of the death of Adam, all I could clearly see was mayhem. I couldn't see or feel any love present. But, as I began the process of sorting out my experiences over the past fourteen years I have grown to see the love of God present in miraculous ways, with messages of forgiveness, hope, and assurance. But I had to stretch myself to understand. Why did Adam die? What did I do? Was it MY fault? How could it have been prevented? These were impossible questions to answer when drowning in a sea of sorrow, confusion and heartache.

As I continue to search for answers, I move closer and closer to God fearfully but with a new, heightened sense of boldness. Adam used to say that the closer he got to God, the more he felt a sense of guilt for the sin in his life. I do, too. However painful, it is where I need to go, into the holy presence of God, for answers that only He has! His response to my cries for help are sometimes painful and often confusing, but they are always healing miracle messages if I look deep.

In the Bible, God says *"Ask and it will be given to you; seek and you will find; knock and the door will be opened to you."* (Matthew 7:7 NIV) Never does He say it will be easy. I take God at His Word. No matter what the pain or trial, I believe Him. I didn't say I understand Him, I only believe. He imparts wisdom, comfort, knowledge and understanding in His time, in His purpose. Trusting God was the most difficult thing I could do at the time, but I tried. And He answered me… with miracles.

Miracles, I have discovered, are simply one of the methods that God uses to communicate with us. Unless we are receptive to the *language* of it, we may miss the message entirely. Have you ever seen two deaf persons talking with their hands? Did you understand what they were saying? Unless you can read sign language the answer is most likely *"No."* But, if you were to learn sign language you would then be able to decipher what the gestures mean. You would begin to understand. The same is true with understanding God's miracles when they occur.

One thing that I have discovered about miracles is that they are NOT coincidences. Someone was quoted as saying that coincidence is simply a miracle where God insists on remaining anonymous. I like that. I believe in miracles... not coincidence.

In sharing my story, my hope is to offer ways for grieving parents, and others, to look for messages from God that bring answers to their questions, healing to their broken hearts, and provide an understanding of how to build a trust in Him, amidst the terrible horror of their lives. The love of God really does come through... the love that never fails. Miracles are evidence of His love.

As a grieving parent I encourage you to be patient in your grief, render yourself to the one-day-at-a-time protection policy. Seek plenty of help from Christian counselors and friends to help you sort out the mystery of what you are going through. Be kind to yourself and to those closest to you, especially your spouse and family.

Take time to heal, and don't worry... you will NEVER forget your love for the one who has died. It will never happen. They will ALWAYS be with you. Forever!

Love is patient. Love is kind. It does not envy, it does not boast, it is not proud. It is not rude, it is not self-seeking, it is not easily angered, it keeps no record of wrongs. Love does not delight in evil, but rejoices with the truth. It always protects, always trusts, always hopes, always perseveres.

Love Never Fails.

1 Corinthians 13:4-8 (NIV)

Three Miracles of God's Love

My Wife Linda

My loving wife Linda, Katrina's mom, Adam's mom, who has remained steadfast in her faith in God, loyal to her family, a woman of character, integrity, and strength of spirit, who demonstrates the kind of love that God desires in all of us, the kind of love that perseveres and suffers long, the love that never fails. Thank you sweetie, for your love.

My Daughter Katrina

From the very day you were born you filled my heart with a sense of delight and wonder. You came into my world invited, and birthed a desire in me to love in ways I never knew I could. I became a daddy. Until I met you I was merely a man. You alone, with no help from the outside world, turned me into a father, a position of lofty pride and dignified status. Your character has not changed throughout your beautiful life. With the strength of a hurricane you challenged the world you entered on the very day of your birth, and you have never wavered from your possession of it. You have become the woman I always envisioned you to be:

1

independent, strong, wise and loving. I thank God for the gift of your life, Katrina. I am eternally blessed to call you my daughter and truly my best friend. I love you.

My Son Adam

Through the fiery trials of your life you emerged a victor, a champion. Your love of life, family and God were the hallmarks of your precious being. Your legacy of mercy, kindness and indelible strength of character lives in the hearts and minds of those whose lives you touched. Your talents were a gift. Your skill in executing them was a testament of your warrior-like heart, fighting your way to excellence and perfection. Your life became like light, a light that continues to draw into it the lives of others in the name of love. I loved our brief time together on earth, as father and son. Thank you for teaching me how to fly and *"...slip the surly bonds of earth to touch the face of God."* Whenever I fly I know you are with me. Thank you, Father God, for the treasure of my son. I'll see you in Heaven Trippy. I love you.

~~~~~~~~~~~~

Here now is my true story...

CHAPTER ONE

Adam

My son

"Push, Linda. It won't be long now. Just keep pushing," said the doctor in the delivery room. The pain of delivery was overcome at the delightful sound of a newborn's crying voice. *"It's a boy!"* they shouted with delight. *"First a beautiful daughter and now a son,"* I thought. We were so happy.

Linda held her newborn son ever so briefly before he was rushed off to be cleaned up by the nurses. She was finally relieved from this trying pregnancy and all it challenged her with and so now it was time to rest. She took a long breath, smiled and kissed me before she drifted off to sleep where she rested from her long labor. Adam Mark Triplett was born on April 24, 1974.

Soon after Adam was born he began to have problems with pain, for about six months. He suffered with what we thought was severe colic or

3

acid reflux but now are convinced that he was allergic to milk. He was constantly crying, particularly after eating. Nothing we did would relieve his suffering. The doctors had no solution either. Nothing helped. Adam suffered. We suffered.

I remember Linda sitting on the retaining wall of a house across the street weeping from fatigue and agonizing over a sense of hopelessness about his pain. I'm sure she felt like a failure as a mother. But, no one knew what to do to make Adam feel better, not even his doctor. Linda was an excellent mother!

We would give him a drop of peppermint oil to soothe his tender tummy, something the doctor had suggested. It only made him cry more. We would take him out for a drive late at night to see if he could fall asleep in the car, and it worked, sometimes. However temporary, it worked.

This went on for nearly six months when suddenly, almost as quickly as his suffering started, it stopped and he seemed healed of whatever ailed him. He began to crawl around, looking for ways to grow. Day-by-day he became more of a delight. There were no more painful tears, only wonder, exploration and discovery. We were so relieved, for us and for him.

As Adam grew he developed a strong, stubborn will to accomplish things, whether it was mastering the puzzle-toys he had or simply walking, running or riding a bike. As he grew, Adam made it his mission in life to conquer the challenge he was faced with, whatever it was.

With the concentration of a heart-surgeon and the stamina of a long-distance runner, Adam would always succeed in his goals. By the time Adam turned five years old he had developed a definite strength in his character and sweet charm.

He also had learned to live life to its full. If something were of interest to him, Adam would pursue it. If it was something he found exciting or challenging, Adam conquered it.

In June of 1979, we attended a picnic with our local church family in Lake Elmo, MN. It was there at the picnic that Adam was introduced to the wonder of flight. A friend from the small church we attended was at the picnic with us and we learned that he owned an airplane. Graciously, he offered to take us up for a ride that sunny afternoon.

I took Adam along, placing him in the front seat where he could see first hand what flying an airplane was like. He was only five years old. When we landed he ran excitedly across the tarmac of the airport to his mom (he always confirmed anything important with his mom first). Out of breath from running and with wide-eyed delight he stated emphatically that when he grew up he wanted to be a pilot. He had discovered his purpose and passion in life. Adam would be a pilot.

Linda and I nurtured his passion and desire to become a pilot by taking him to air shows when possible, presenting him with birthday and holiday gifts that were of the aviation theme, and when traveling we informed the flight crew that Adam was going to be a pilot when he grew up. The captain always made an announcement like, *"Ladies and gentlemen, this is the captain speaking... and we want to welcome a future pilot who is on board today, Mr. Adam Triplett. Welcome aboard Adam."* Adam would beam with assurance and confidence while blushing with delight for all the attention. Yes, Adam would most certainly become an airplane pilot one day.

In our neighborhood, the children would get together and play Kids' Parades, and that's where Adam would easily go into character like a seasoned method actor. Many times he would pretend to be a pilot, stretching his arms wide and with pursed lips make a "brbrbrbrbrbrbrbr" sound, as if he were a 747 with Pratt & Whitney engines. Interestingly, that little engine sound-making practice would come in handy later in life in Adam's musical endeavor. Kids' Parades were something the kids conjured up and did often on the spur of the moment to pass their time away during the day. Almost all of the children participated with wagons, tricycles, even baby walkers. It was a delight to watch all these young children entertain themselves (and us) with a parade. The parade route was usually no longer than two or three houses where they would turn around and parade back.

Adam would live the character he dressed up to impersonate. It could be Robin of the Batman fame, a cowboy, telephone repairman, or even Alex Keaton from the 1970s TV show "Family Ties", whatever it was, Adam immersed himself in the character. In fact, the Alex Keaton character was suit-cased on our trek to Rochester, MN. We were relocated due to my job with the phone company. In September of 1979 I had been promoted to a management position in Rochester, and when we moved, "Alex" came along. I think he actually became Adam's alter ego of sorts.

Once in Rochester, Adam entered the public school system at the age of five. Every teacher fell in love with Adam (and his secret friend Alex). As time went on Adam began to have difficulty with his studies, particularly with completing assignments and concentration in class.

His teachers felt that Adam was a bright little boy, certainly one who knew and understood the subjects he was being taught. Many of them simply accommodated Adam by accepting only part of the work required to complete an assignment. We believe Alex had a part in it as well.

His sweet nature and adorable charm eventually got him into trouble by not having to work hard in his studies. By second grade, Adam began to struggle more and more, and eventually not even his cute little friend Alex could bail him out. Adam was on a downward slide academically and there was talk of putting him into a Special Ed class for children with learning disabilities.

Linda would have nothing of it. Adam was a smart little boy who had been given far too much leeway and now suffered for it.

It was in 1981 that as a young boy of only seven years old Adam showed serious signs of struggling with school and with learning in general. Math was particularly difficult for him. Although he tried, he continued to struggle to master math.

As parents, we strained to find solutions for him, as did his educators. Discipline was not a problem, since Adam's behaviors were always polite and respectful. He behaved very well and honestly gave us no trouble. We were stumped.

One day while shopping at a local department store, we came across a sale of small computers (the Texas ti99-4A to be exact). This was to be the very first of many computers to enter the home of the Triplett family, and would prove to be not only a wise investment but also one that would guide Adam in his struggles in math (and general studies) toward success and with it opened a world of opportunity for him to learn.

This little computer had games and what little boy doesn't like computer games? Well, some of these games involved – math problems. As Adam played, and he played very hard, he became more and more adept to understanding how math worked.

Without realizing it, Adam was finding a learning process within himself. He finally found the door of learning, opened it and entered a brave new world. And as the skilled surgeon and long-distance runner in him would have it, Adam dove in head long to educating himself as only Adam could do. He began working very hard on his studies. But it would be years of discovery through hard work, strong efforts and most of all very good teachers before Adam would achieve the highest standing of accomplishments he had set out for. Adam earned it!

It wasn't until we moved from Rochester, MN to White Bear Lake in 1985 that a definite change in Adam's education became more evident. This was in large part due to his sixth-grade teacher, Mr. Denton, who challenged Adam with accepting more responsibility and ownership of his work. In short, Mr. Denton put Adam's feet to the fire and made him complete all of his assignments, and on time. Suffice to say, Mr. Denton was not Adam's favorite teacher... at least not until he could look back as an adult and see how this marvelous teacher sculpted him academically.

Moving from Rochester to White Bear Lake was a difficult transition for Adam. He felt like he was at the bottom socially and academically, except for his musical skills and trumpet playing. I remember meeting with Adam to discuss some of his frustrations with the transition. Most notably was his comment, *"In Rochester I was popular. Kids liked me and so did the teachers. Here [White Bear Lake] no one even knows me, and the teachers are mean."*

In what we learned from Dr. James Dobson's teaching, we knew that Adam's music and trumpet playing could be the one thing to help him adjust. We nurtured his love of aviation and his trumpet playing. In Rochester they started band one year earlier than in White Bear. That gave Adam the head start that was needed to rise above the rest, to shine and build his confidence.

Over the next few years in middle school Adam became a remarkable student and loved learning. By the time he entered his senior year in high school Adam was already on his way to being highly successful in all disciplines of learning.

He prided himself for remembering facts and figures, for memorizing over 150 mathematical theorems, for fun he would read physics books and he loved to enter debates on political issues. He knew the Bible and could handle deep philosophical discussions with seasoned scholars. He easily excelled in his studies, especially in math and music.

As a father I was amazed at Adam's abilities to confront a challenge and conquer it with dignity. He certainly made me proud of his accomplishments, from athletics to academics, as he always reached his goals and beyond. I was humbled by him, this boy of mine. My pride was not so much in the accomplishments of the tasks, but in the building of his character and manhood.

As a father, I watched Adam emerge from a little caterpillar to a beautiful butterfly, flying free and unbounded in his abilities and wonder about life. As a gardener I looked upon his life as the grandest of flowers that I planted, watered and protected from the elements, to produce the award-winning brilliance he revealed to the world.

As parents, Linda and I had agreed very early on that our children would be exposed to music and that each of them would learn to play a musical instrument. It was not an option. They both had a responsibility to learn about and to play a musical instrument. We started them on the piano at early ages, Katrina being seven and Adam five.

Katrina melted into the piano, playing with passion, feeling and intensity. She blossomed. Adam, on the other hand, absolutely hated the thing. Hated it! Recitals were enough to give him headaches and a very grumpy disposition. As a result, he did not last long on the piano. We stuck to our principles about learning music and playing an instrument, so we gave Adam the choice to play another instrument. (Prayerfully we hoped he would not become a drummer.)

Adam chose the trumpet. Naturally, as with any new challenge, there were many times of trial and frustration. Adam suffered often with a split lower lip from working with his horn. However, after he built up his lip strength his problems decreased and he continued to play with determination and passion.

He also struggled with asthma and had to use an inhaler on many occasions. But, with his new joy of learning and finding the link to his inner passion, Adam eventually played that perfect note. From then on it was practice, practice, practice. I believe this is where I lost most of my hearing.

Through his years of hard work and diligent pursuit of excellence, Adam learned to play the trumpet very well. In fact, well enough to be the featured soloist at the 1991-1992 Minnesota All-State Jazz Ensemble, held at Orchestra Hall in Minneapolis when Adam was just 17 years old. After high school Adam played trumpet professionally while beginning to pursue a career in aviation.

In July of 1992, Adam began his flight training at the Inver Hills Community College Aviation Program, in association with Wings, Inc. of St. Paul. It was during that first year at IHCC that Adam enjoyed the tandem ride of aviation and trumpet successes with flight training at Wings, Inc. and his debut of professional trumpet player for The

15

Butanes. I think this combo packed a one-two punch in Adam's desire to fulfill his dreams. Nothing could stop him. He was empowered and willing to work. Eventually, a couple of years at IHCC, Adam made his way to Moody Bible Institute in Chicago, Illinois to study aviation and missions work with the Missions Aviation Fellowship.

Adam found Chicago fascinating with its mixed culture of street people and millionaires all walking down the same sidewalks. He 'jammed' on the streets with locals, polishing his improvisational musical skills. His studies at MBI gave Adam the exposure to see first hand the need to spread the love of God to all he met. His most notable was a man named Anthony.

Anthony was a street person, living literally in a box under a bridge. Anthony had HIV. Adam would visit Anthony from time-to-time and share his faith with him. A tough sell, but Anthony eventually succumbed to Adam's relentless pursuit to lead him to Christ. We believe that Anthony later went on to be with the Lord. I recall Adam telling Linda and me, with tears in his eyes, *"...I will see Anthony in Heaven some day, of that I am sure!"*

Adam returned home from Chicago after one year in the MBI aviation program. MBI missions leaders suggested to Adam that he continue his aviation career outside the missions field, where he could be a greater asset to the missions field as a professional pilot. Adam was disappointed, to say the least. He worked so very hard to fulfill every requirement MBI had made of him. He hadn't failed at anything at all. The MBI professors simply recognized in Adam a greater desire to fly airplanes than be an on-the-ground missionary. Nevertheless, Adam was disappointed with himself and returned to White Bear Lake in 1995.

I explained to Adam that it was not his true calling, to become a missionary who flew, but rather a pilot who could support the mission field by becoming a 'sender' (one who financially supports a missions field or missionary). He seemed quite satisfied with that and could relate to one 'sender' in our local church family, who supported many world missions with financial support. Adam eagerly went back into flying with the same enthusiasm that made him the remarkable man that he was.

Within a few short years Adam had achieved his MEI/CFI (Multi-Engine Instructor / Certified Flight Instructor) license and by March of 1997 Adam became my very own flight Instructor.

I learned a lot from my boy. Most folks think it was the other way around, the father teaching the son. Sure, I did that too, but Adam taught me how to extend love for others, by really living it out. He humbled me often. I remember the day Adam was accepted as a professional Certified Flight Instructor and employed by Wings, Inc. of St. Paul. Wings, Inc. was considered one of the premier flight schools in the five-state area, second only to North Dakota University's Aerospace program. Adam earned his MEI/CFI rating in February of 1997 and was hired by Wings, Inc. soon after.

I began flying with Adam as a student in March. I had not completed my flight training with him before he was killed in the tragic accident on August 4, 1997. However, he did get to see me fly solo and complete my first cross-country flight.

I know I made him proud, and along with earning his living as a flight Instructor at Wings, Inc. in St. Paul, he had achieved his dream of becoming a pilot and a professional musician.

I think if Adam were writing about his life it would sound very much like this...

My Aviation Career...

My very first airplane ride was at a church picnic in Lake Elmo on June 29, 1979. I was only five years old. We flew out of the Lake Elmo (21D) airport in the northeast suburbs of St. Paul, MN. I actually got to sit in the front seat, next to the pilot, Mr. Jim Bristol. The airplane we flew was a Cessna 180 'Tail-dragger', N1737C.

I remember the excitement of taking off and flying high above the people. Mr. Bristol was a friend of my mom and dad, and he asked me if I wanted to take the controls, to actually fly the airplane myself. "Yes" I said and I grabbed the yoke (that's the steering wheel) and immediately I became a pilot in my heart. Mr. Bristol showed me how to bank left and right, how to make the plane go up and down, and even gave me the thrill of feeling a little weightless. It was so cool!

When we landed I remember jumping out of the cockpit (that's what they call the place where the pilot sits), and I ran to my mom (she looked a little worried) and I told her that when I grew up I wanted to be a pilot.

19

Music and My Trumpet…

    I began my musical career with piano lessons at the ripe age of five. I hated it! I couldn't sit still long enough to find any interest with the darned thing. I liked music sure enough, but the piano was NOT for me. I tried and tried to learn to play well but just didn't find a place in my heart for it. My parents told me that if I was able to finish at least one recital I could choose to play any instrument other than piano, but I HAD to learn to play something. I chose the trumpet.

    I started learning to play the trumpet at the age of eight. My dad used to tease me about my earlier playing days by telling me he could make better music swinging the family cat over his head. I was not amused. I was determined to prove him wrong about all that cat stuff and so I practiced, and practiced, and practiced. My dad eventually lost most of his hearing, and as for Rikki Tikki Tavi, our family cat, well he finally issued a huge sigh of relief and eventually came out of hiding.

    In high school I played for the school orchestra, school band, and the school jazz band. It was here that I found my real love of this marvelous instrument. Focusing on classical, jazz and R&B styles of music, I quickly excelled in playing the trumpet. I was able to convince my parents that in order for me to play my best, I needed the best in an instrument. After hearing one of my first concerts they agreed, and soon I became the very proud owner of a beautiful, new silver Besson trumpet.

Continuing to practice each day, sometimes with a cracked lip, I gained enough confidence to enter the Minnesota High School Music Competition in 1991. I placed first in the jazz trumpet soloist competition and the following summer I was off to Jazz Camp. I eventually won the Luis Armstrong Award For Excellence. I was on cloud ninety-nine!

That same year, 1991-1992, I was a featured artist on trumpet at the Minnesota State Jazz Ensemble held at Orchestra Hall in Minneapolis, and I received a standing ovation for my performance (well, at least from my family).

Following high school, I played professionally for a local R&B group known as The Butanes. Most of our gigs were in the Twin Cities, but we managed from time-to-time to perform in Nebraska, Iowa and Wisconsin. After a year or so with The Butanes, and having spent my post high school time attending Inver Hills Community College in the Aviation Program, I decided to attend Moody Bible Institute in Chicago, Illinois.

In Chicago, I often played my trumpet on the city streets jamming with local talent whenever possible. I also played in a group formed by the Moody Music Department (mostly for school functions). Some of my favorites professional trumpet artists, and real inspirations to me, are Winton Marsalis, Doc Severinsen,

Phil Driscoll, Maynard Ferguson, and of course the famous Louis Armstrong.

My Besson now sits silent, waiting for my return with Jesus. And I will return with Him one day. He promised it in His Word. Some of my family and Christian friends believe that I may even 'sound the trumpet call' at the return of Jesus to the earth. It could happen. At any rate, are you ready for when He does return? If not, please don't wait. Accept Jesus as your Savior now. Be assured of your life after death. I did.

Adam grew up in a Christian home, much like the one I grew up in. He accepted Jesus as his Savior at the age of seventeen, and in keeping with his style of learning, he excelled in his faith and studied the Bible constantly. After one year at MBI Adam returned home, filled with the Word of God in his heart and a lifetime's worth of experience in serving others in Chicago.

Shortly after returning to Minnesota, Adam was asked by our pastor to preach a sermon on a Sunday when he would be out-of-town. Adam was thrilled (and a bit nervous) about the whole thing and in keeping with everything else he did, he went all-out and decided to preach a sermon from Genesis to Revelation. However, guided by the pastor's wisdom in such matters, Adam settled with "love" being the foundation of his message.

Adam felt love was the foundation of everything good. In fact, he memorized the entire love chapter of the Bible, 1 Corinthians 13. And even though his sermon traveled back and forth from Genesis to Revelation, he maintained the basis of it in "love".

Adam's baptism with Pastor Metzger

Throughout the short twenty-three years of his life, Adam demonstrated a remarkable sense of being alive. Everything in life filled him with wonder and beckoned his investigation and exploration. He was in love with life. Music, politics, mathematics, science, religion and romance... they all filled his passion for being alive. He drank it in with fervor. Everything Adam did he did with purpose.

In April of 1997, just after his 23rd birthday, Adam married the love of his life, well one of them. Whenever Adam dated a girl, his intent was to show her honest love, respect and adoration. His ability and desire to love was noted among the girls that knew him. Adam had many female friends and only a few serious romances along the way.

Adam was always looking ahead, planning for that one day in the future when he would find the right one to settle down and marry. I remember Adam asking me how to know, how to be sure it was the right girl. His ability to love, nurture and show respect for people fueled the question, I believe. He wanted to make the right choice for his and for her sake. *"Dad, how can I know if she is the right one? How did you know?"* I told him about how I met his mom, Linda...

I was in the 9th grade entering 10th. We met at a school function where my rock band was the entertainment. (Ok, it was a school dance). I was the lead singer in what we wanted to be known as a Rock Band. Unfortunately, we missed the mark not in our music, but in our marketing. Someone (who will remain nameless here) decided the name of our all-male band should be... The Tiaras! I didn't even know what a tiara was at first. Here I was, a gymnast and football player for the high school and I was the lead singer in a band called The

Tiaras – a princess crown. Ugh! Well, back to Adam's question. I told Adam that during a break at the dance I went outside to get some fresh air and cool off a bit (from all the Mick Jagger-like gyrations). That's when I saw Linda, standing just inside the entry of the junior high school (today they are called Middle School).

There she was, beyond beauty, something from the gods. The moment I saw her, everything around her went dark, like I was in slow motion looking through a telescope from a distance. All I could focus on was her face, her incredibly beautiful face. I had no awareness of anyone else being present, although I could hear faint voices. I think they were voices. It didn't matter. All I could do to keep breathing was to ignore all else and keep my eyes on her. I was stunned, electrified, smitten.

Adam seemed to hang on every word as if I were revealing secrets from ages past. He didn't say a word. I continued…

In what seemed like an eternity I struggled even to breathe. Eventually, after a moment or two, she slowly looked up at me, quite gently and gave me a smile that shot through my heart like an arrow from a champion archer. I fell into her eyes, deep and dark and filled with mystery and promise. I was in love.

I didn't know it at the time but what I was experiencing was passionate, longing, enduring love. I

25

surrendered to her immediately. I could not resist. I wouldn't resist.

For Adam it proved to be the right advice. I remember telling him that he would know in his heart, mind and soul when the right one comes along. And it happened to him exactly as it did to me, the first time he saw the girl of his dreams. Her name is Karin.

Adam was out with the staff and flight instructors from Wings, Inc. after work one evening, celebrating the promotion of one of their own to Mesaba Airlines. That's when he saw Karin.

26

From across the room he noticed her. He told me that the very moment their eyes met the room went dark, as if he were looking at her through a telescope and sounds of faint voices filled the room.

It was not long after that Adam and Karin were a couple, destined for the alter. They were married on April 26, 1997 just two days after his 23rd birthday.

They spent their honeymoon traveling up to the North Shore of Minnesota visiting the Split Rock Lighthouse, Gooseberry Falls and lodging on the shores of Lake Superior in Duluth, MN.

They were blissfully happy. They were in love! I remember meeting Karin for the first time. She was soft spoken, petite, delicate in form and delightfully feminine. I could immediately see the attraction Adam had. She was beautiful, with soft, light brown hair and big, brown eyes.

She was a bit shy and quiet, but behind those eyes was a mind as sharp as any chef's knife. Quick-witted, but stealthy in her delivery, almost over our heads at times, she blended in effortlessly with all of us. Karin had a small tattoo on the back of her shoulder. Thumper, the bunny of Disney fame. It fit her to a tee. Energetic, happy, innocent and all wrapped up in a cuddly sweet girl.

It was interesting watching her blend into our family, as if we had already met. She was shy, yet bold. Her voice was soft and sweet, even when she was trying to sound tough, which wasn't very often. Actually, I never heard her once raise her voice. She exhibited a stately calm demeanor, always self-assured but never self-centered. Her ability to love our Adam was transparent.

She was in love with Adam and every gesture proclaimed it. He too was smitten, with smiles that lasted hours and breathing that seemed labored when she was near. He adored the fact that she aspired to be a stay-at-home mom, just like his mom had done, and had done it so very well.

Their love was passionate, rich with wonder and filled with delight. I could tell she was absolutely the right girl for him. I knew it in my heart. I could see it in Adam's eyes. *"Adam and Karin"*… it sounded perfect, like it was one single name.

In the midst of the beauty and bliss of seeing our son, now a grown man, happily married, never could we have predicted the mayhem that was now fast approaching our lives…

CHAPTER TWO

Mark

Adam's Dad

I grew up in St. Paul, Minnesota, in a large Christian family of eleven, nine children and my parents. I am third from the oldest, having seven brothers and one sister... David, Rebecca, *Mark*, Daniel, Paul, John, James, Timothy, and Michael. The environment I grew up in was rather chaotic (nine children!). We were what most people today would consider poor, although we never went to bed hungry and always had clean clothes to wear to school.

My dad had attended the Cincinnati Bible College for ministry work, early in his life. During World War II he served as Chaplain's Assistant in a prison camp just outside of London. Upon returning from the war he began building a family, starting with David and ending with Michael. My brothers, David and Michael, are 20 years apart.

Finding employment with Honeywell and later the U.S. Postal Service, dad worked very hard to take good care of us. We rarely missed church on Sunday and whenever anyone would come to visit, the topic of conversation soon drifted toward biblical themes, usually the book of Revelation and end times prophesy.

My dad also fancied himself a mystery writer and actually published a few small examples of his work. He spent quite a number of years writing his 1500 page mystery novel, complete with characters from his life-long pursuit of success, all done on an old typewriter. Dad died at the age of 87, two years after Adam's death. Sadly, dad's novel went unpublished.

My mom started out being the quintessential stay-at-home mom, raising her nine children in a three-bedroom home. Later, she landed a job with the 3M Company, where she spent 30 years working full-time to help support her large family.

As a young girl, my mother played the violin, although not enough to become a professional musician. She also was an English teacher for a brief time, in Webster City, Iowa, her hometown. My mother was a very hard worker, constantly attending to her brood. When she wasn't working at

3M, she could be found in the kitchen cooking us a meal or in the basement at the ringer-washer toiling with piles of dirty laundry. Summer days were punctuated with a continual supply of clothes hanging on the line in the back yard. Oh, diapers were made of cloth back then and there was no such thing as a diaper service. My mom slaved over us.

Mom grew up in Webster City, Iowa along with three sisters; Mary Margaret, Mary Jean and Shirley. She and her sisters meet annually for a reunion of *"The Four Iowa Broads."* That's what they call themselves. Back in 2008 I was asked to photograph those sultry sisters for a calendar spread. No, it wasn't anything found in the stores, it was just for themselves and a few family members and friends. It was a hoot!

My mom is one of the best cooks in the world. Her Sunday pot-roast is legendary and her glazed ham... well, "yum" doesn't even scratch the surface of our praise to her cooking. Sundays were a great time together with family, even if it was chaotic. We were a large family, with some quirks but none-the-less a strongly bonded family, rooted in the love and care of dedicated parents who lived out their faith in God.

With my siblings I learned to be creative at an early age. As I said, we were poor, and had to make do with whatever we had. It was fine for my siblings and me; we didn't know the difference at all. We played in the dirt, made forts out of old doors and tree branches, pretended to be super-heroes like Zorro and Superman.

It would not be uncommon for neighbors to see a stream of Triplett boys flash by their front windows each adorned with dish towels tied around their necks as capes. October nights were the very best, each of us being our own version of Zorro. We would break branches from Mrs. Behrens's lilac bushes for our swords, sharpen the tips with my mom's turkey carving knife, and ride off under the full moon on the back of our invisible black stallions, leaving the famous "Z" scratched in the dirt just like the real Zorro would have done. We didn't care that we all played the same character. We loved the part and ran ourselves to exhaustion each night. We slept like babies.

As a young boy I played baseball and a little football with the neighborhood playground teams. In junior high school I began a more serious endeavor – gymnastics, where I excelled. By the ninth grade I had won many first place awards and followed it up by attending the Minnesota State High School Gymnastics Tournament in 1969, my senior year. It was a proud moment in my young life, one of the significant things that had helped shape me into the man I was to become. During my years in senior high school I also played on the football team as a running back and multiple defense positions. I loved sports. But, I actually loved the wilderness more.

As I said earlier, I met Linda at a school dance, back in the fall of 1965. We dated for the remainder of that school year but when summer came I left her for the Boundary Waters in Northern Minnesota and Canada... for three months!

If I were to tell you what my actual *"first love"* was, it would most certainly have to be the Boundary Waters Canoe Area Wilderness (BWCAW). That summer in 1966 was a much-needed break from city life and the chaos of my large family with all of its sibling rivalries. The YMCA wilderness camp, Camp Widjiwagan, would be both my refuge from city life and a real boot-camp type of experience, one that would change me from a boy to a man. Camp Widjiwagan is situated on the north arm of Burntside Lake, just a few miles from Ely, MN.

From there, I trekked into the BWCAW on long canoe trips deep into Canada where few people have traveled. My longest trip into the BWCAW was a 21-day trip deep into the interior of Canada's wilderness with hundreds of miles of canoeing, portaging and even hopping a ride on the Canadian

Pacific railroad into Kenora, about 25 miles north of the tip of Minnesota at Lake of the Woods.

My summer at Camp Widjiwagan was an experience of a lifetime. I was blessed with meaningful work and I found the presence of God in the beauty and silence of the north woods. I had been a born-again Christian since the age of twelve, and I believe I was saved at that time. But it was not until my experience there that summer at camp that I ever met the holy presence of my God. It was there I heard the voice of God for the first time, in the quiet solitude of his creation.

That summer up north, while experiencing the opportunity of a lifetime, I also found the pain associated with love. I pined for my girl back in St. Paul. I was in love with two opposing mistresses. One was my Linda, warm and sweet smelling who could kiss away any concerns I may have. The other was my wilderness job, an ogre that worked me from sunrise to sunset, willing to spill my guts on jagged rocks while racing down rapids of some uncharted river in Canada, but offering me the peace, serenity and beauty of the wilderness I so loved. Both were alluring, both satisfying and both demanding on my soul.

I gave way to the stronger pull of the mistress of the wild north woods and when I returned to St. Paul three months later I was a young man changed by the forces of nature, both within and without. I would painfully learn the fate of my decision to leave Linda, a beautiful sixteen-year-old girl, alone on summer vacation. She had left me for another.

I was mortally wounded, to my core. My sister Becky would drive me past Linda's home late at night just so I might get a glimpse of her. Hanging out the car window I would call her name. *"Linda!"* I always cried on the way home. There were only a couple of those trips that Becky would be willing to make. She quickly decided she had much better things to do with her time so she cancelled further car rides.

After that, throughout my three years in senior high school, I only dated a few girls, landing on one in particular which lasted about a year. It was a tumultuous relationship to say the least. She was NOT even close to the perfection of my Linda. Although everyone who knew me thought I would marry that other girl, they would soon discover that they were wrong. My heart belonged to Linda Langton and I was determined to get her back.

I dated some while in high school but the echo of Linda resonated in my heart. I compared every girl to her. Although I met some awesome girls in my young life there was only one who could fill my heart with joy...Linda. I had dated one girl for a few years and all my friends and family were convinced we would marry one day. We broke up shortly after graduation and went our separate ways.

It was then, at the urging of my friend Marty, that I mustered up the courage to give Linda Langton a call. I can remember to this day how dry my mouth was, how nervous I felt just hearing her voice over the phone.

"Hi Linda, it's Mark Triplett. Remember me?" I was sure she was already seeing someone, probably better looking, more rugged and likely engaged to be married. *"Oh, hi Mark. What a wonderful surprise...I was just thinking about you the other day..."* The normal pre-date dialogue continued until we found ourselves making a date for Friday night.

We spent the next few months getting reacquainted with each other and being more mature than three years earlier we found ourselves interested in more of who we were and what our dreams could be. That evolved into a blending of our hearts once again, weaving our life's dreams together into one.

In January of 1970 I asked Linda Langton to be my wife.

We were married in a beautiful old Methodist church on the East Side of St. Paul in June of that same year. The two had now become one. That was over 41 years ago, as of this writing.

Yes, I married the only love of my life, Linda Sue Langton, about a year after graduating high school. As I stated in the previous chapter, I fell head-over-heels in love with her in October of 1965, when I was in the ninth grade, and I asked her to marry me in 1970 just a few months after graduation. I was just 18 year old. We were married on June 6, 1970 and later had two beautiful children, Katrina and Adam.

Our first child came two years after being married, in 1972. Her name is Katrina Lynn, and she entered the world feisty and ready to take on anyone who dare stand in her way. She was a whopping five-pound three-ounces of daring little girl and I couldn't wait to see what she would grow into. I deeply fell in love a second time.

Katrina became a whole new world for me to discover. When I close my eyes and think back to those days when she was a tiny infant, I can feel her warm little body cradled in my arms, close to my heart. I would listen to her breathe with a squeaky little sound. She was petite, yet powerful. I could already sense it. Many years later she would have a hurricane named after her. Aptly named as well.

I love my daughter! She is so beautiful, very wise and indelibly strong. A woman now, she measures only 5'5", but she pushes thousand-pound horses around like they were made of hay. Katrina is truly another wonderful miracle of God's love. She and Adam were the absolute best of friends and the closest of siblings. She was the big sister Adam needed to help develop his character and build his lasting legacy. She is now a grown woman, a wife and mother of principled ethics, tempered resilience, and lasting fortitude. She is gentle and sweet, valiant and brave. She never backs down from a fight but never starts one. We call her Trina.

My career aspiration after graduating from St. Paul Johnson Sr. High School was to enter law enforcement as a police officer. I served as a volunteer police reserve officer for the city of Maplewood, MN for about four years, from 1974 to 1978, hoping it would lead to a permanent position. During that same period of time, I also served as an observer with the Minnesota State Patrol, riding with Trooper Michael Haines. I attended Lakewood Community College in classes for law enforcement, although at the time it was not a requirement to have any college-level training to become a police officer. I earned my AA degree from Lakewood Community College (now named Century College), and later my BA in Business Communications from Concordia College, St. Paul.

In 1976, I was invited to join the honorable ranks of the Minnesota State Patrol as a Trooper. I had passed all the tests and was now being accepted into their elite ranks. I was actually seeing my dream come true. Joy! Not only would I become a law enforcement officer, but I was being invited to join the ranks of what I considered to be the elite in law enforcement – the Minnesota State Patrol. Elation set in, but it was very short-lived. My dream, having come to reality after all that hard work was now to be crushed by the decision of a single state official who prevented me from following that dream. The reason: the color of my skin. Reverse discrimination seemed to be the root cause of the decision to deny me acceptance into the State Patrol. I was a white male, an unpopular breed back in the 1970s.

About a year later that same State official that denied me a job was discharged from his employment by the State of Minnesota for reasons of discrimination, but by then it was a lost cause for me. I would never see my dream come true. It was the mid 1970s, a hard time in our history when being politically sensitive was just coming onto the radar of our cultural vocabulary. I had given my very best for over four years to achieve my dream but it still seemed hopeless. I could study, to no avail. I could volunteer weekends and nights to learn and gain experience, but it didn't seem to matter. I could not be anything other than be a white male.

I was hurt and angry but I could find no resolve, since not one law firm in the Twin Cities of Minneapolis and St. Paul would take my case. They all told me it was too politically sensitive, with no hope of actually winning the case. No one would offer any help at all. Feeling abandoned, I decided to just give it up and move on, to choose a different path. I had worked so hard to achieve my dream and now had no choice but to accept the fact that I could not fight prejudice. Angry and hurt, I moved on.

Armed with a passion unfulfilled, I began to pursue a management position with my employer, Northwestern Bell Telephone Company, where I had worked since graduating from high school in 1969. I worked very hard. I worked long hours. I excelled and found advancement and was promoted to a management position in 1979.

I was proud of my accomplishments but enjoyed the glory of it for only a very short time. My promotion had relocated our family from the Twin Cities to Rochester, MN in 1979 where I became the Regional Supervisor to the Materials Management organization, serving Rochester and the SE quarter of the state.

With enthusiasm I went to work each day, discovering new challenges and the growth that came with it. However, I soon discovered that it would not be easy; since I was looked upon as an outsider, from *the big city* and found prejudice came in many forms. This time it was territorial. Good grief!

I had only been on my new assignment for a couple of years when the breakup of the Bell System began to occur. In 1983 the Bell System was divested and a new era of telecommunications was about to emerge. And with it, I faced the increasing pressures of life and, and at times I felt overwhelmed by the challenges, and unfairness that saturated my job. I always worried about losing my job. Some days I just wanted to hide.

Earlier in my career with the phone company I had worked outside on the phone poles and in manholes, inside testing centers and central offices and even in-and-out of people's homes as a telephone repairman. I loved it! I was meeting new people and having a wide diversity of work to do.

In management, I worked in a wide variety of service and support fields but found most of them dissatisfying and too political. I found the politics of being in management a bit distasteful, but I hung in there determined to make the best of any situation. Computers and the Internet were fast approaching in the mid 1980s as the newest era of telecommunications, and an exciting new opportunity was on the horizon. I delved into it with an Adam-like fervor.

After the breakup of the Bell System I was forced to relocate my family again, this time from Rochester, MN back to the Twin Cities, where we eventually found a new home in White Bear Lake. Jobs were being eliminated at an alarming rate in the company and my first assignment after moving from Rochester was to locate and acquire a new position, since my old position was being eliminated. They gave me six months. They could have simply laid me off, but the company provided me with an opportunity to seek and find a new position within. I was grateful and looking back can clearly see the grace of God in it. It took hard work and many face-to-face interviews, but I eventually found myself working in Minneapolis in a systems support group.

It was on that job where, for the first time in my life, I would discover the raw face of evil first hand. All of my previous trials up to that point were child's play compared to what lay ahead. I felt doomed. It seemed that my new boss was determined to eliminate me from the position, if not even from the company, since she was given no authority in my hiring. Very quickly, I learned that she held nothing but distain for me. I couldn't understand why. She vowed to ruin my career and have me removed not only from the job, but from the company as well.

Nothing I did would sway her from her relentless attacks. For reasons I still do not know, she pursued me with a death grip crushing my hope of keeping my employment. I struggled to cope and within a year was diligently looking for another assignment, anything to rid myself of her evil plans.

By the grace of God, I landed in what was known as a Strategic Account, one that carried the multi-million dollar stressors associated with it. I worked hard to make a good impression on my boss, co-workers and most importantly, the customer, and I received awards from both. I enjoyed my tenure with that account and worked with an Adam-like enthusiasm.

It was a tough job, this multi-million dollar account, but there were great times of satisfaction and accomplishment. I grew into the digital age quickly working there. The wrongs of my life seemed to be fading into the past with a bright hope on the horizon.

I was working a respectable job close to home, making a decent salary, one that would be greatly needed to provide for my family and to pay for Adam's schooling and flight training. The world seemed a bit brighter, more secure. I decided to make the best of what I had been given and asked Adam to teach me to fly airplanes. In March of 1997, I entered the world of flight, with Adam at my side as my flight instructor. I too would be a pilot of airplanes. My son would teach me.

Adam was impressed with my flying skills and eagerness to do my very best. I was so proud of him, and I wanted him to be as proud of me. We flew dozens of training flights over the St. Croix river-valley that separates Minnesota and Wisconsin. He would test my knowledge and ability to control the airplane and to his surprise and delight, I did. I studied very hard since I knew he would not accept anything short of my very best. And, I gave it to him. Although he never told me directly, he did confide in Linda "...*dad is an awesome pilot!*" It didn't matter how I heard it, it was music to my ears.

During one flight lesson Adam asked if I would like to experience *"zero gravity."* I enthusiastically said yes. Taking the controls, Adam made the airplane climb up to 5000 feet where he sharply pushed the nose forward and headed into a shallow, controlled dive. All unsecured items in the cabin of the aircraft became weightless. As a pen floated past us I flicked it to spin, like the propeller of the plane. It was an awesome experience.

When Adam pulled up to bring the aircraft back to level flight I experienced 3g's of weight. We headed back to the airport, where he continued to test my alertness and skills by forcing me to do an emergency landing on a different runway. I passed with flying colors (pun intended).

There were two flights with Adam that I remember with deep intimacy and bonding. One was on June 14, 1997. It was a cross-country flight from St. Paul's Holman Field, our base of operation, to Eau Claire, Wisconsin and back to St. Paul. It was a night flight and the moon was full with a clear sky – a perfect night for flying.

We talked about many things during that flight, mostly about flight training and his dreams of becoming a commercial pilot at a large airline one day. It was on that flight Adam thanked me for all that Linda and I had done for him.

I was so proud of him and he expressed the same with me. We rode in silence for a while, with a full moon reflecting on the lakes and streams below. It was a most special moment, between a father and his son.

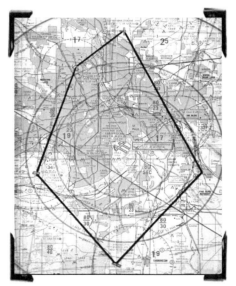

"Round Robin" flight

Another very memorable flight with Adam was the **Round Robin**, on July 6,1997, just one month before Adam would pass from this life to his eternal rest with God. The Round Robin was an airport-to-airport flight surrounding the Twin Cities, including airports at St. Paul, Anoka-Blaine, Crystal, Flying Cloud, and Farmington airports.

It was another night flight operation and one that finalized my training with him. I was so pleased and proud of my son, and now I could share with him his love of aviation, a desire born from a flight long ago when he was a little boy attending a church picnic. We talked about one day opening a flight school together, one where I could manage and he would teach. Sadly, that dream would never come true. The mayhem was about to begin.

On August 4, 1997, I found myself in a deep emotional and spiritual ditch, once again experiencing extreme self-pity for the injustices in my life. I found myself losing a grip on my joy, being coerced into a defensive posture from increasing pressures at work.

I hated seeing myself like this and ached in my heart to have the joy return. It didn't. With an attitude of arrogance, pride and a haughty spirit I found myself arguing with God regarding an issue of sin in my life at the time. At a low point of my character, I argued with God about my attitude and behaviors that day, and I challenged Him with *"...and what are you going to do [about it] God, kill my son...?"* The moment I said it I wished I could take it back, but it was too late. That was the day Adam would die, and I was about to witness the greatest horror of my life as the mayhem began…

*"The thief [satan] comes only to
steal, kill and destroy…"*

John 10:10 (NIV)

CHAPTER THREE

Mayhem

The Thief

Monday, August 4, 1997

3:15 pm

"*New Richmond traffic, Duchess one-eight-niner-six-zero departing runway three-two. Any traffic in the area please advise, New Richmond,*" Adam announced over the radio.

Adam loved flying. His dream since age five was to be a pilot. Now, at the age of twenty-three he was not only a professional pilot, but a certified flight instructor as well. He held a Multi-Engine Instrument rating as an instructor (MEI/CFI). He had flown nearly 800 hours total time, over 100 of which were in the Duchess, a twin-engine trainer. He was working very hard toward being hired by Mesaba or Northwest Airlines very soon. Just a few

49

more hours were needed to meet hiring requirements.

"New Richmond traffic, Duchess one-eight-niner-six-zero entering a left cross-wind for runway three-two remaining in the pattern. All traffic please advise, New Richmond."

The weather was ideal for flying. Temperatures were in the mid 80s, no clouds, and only a slight breeze out of the northwest, straight down the runway. It was a perfect day to fly. Actually, any day was "perfect" for flying as far as Adam was concerned. It was just more perfect that day.

"New Richmond traffic, Duchess one-eight-niner-six-zero entering a left down-wind for runway three-two. New Richmond."

The Duchess – N18960

10:00 am that same day…

I had received a call from Linda early that morning, at my office. She told me that Adam had lost his keys to his Ford Ranger and wondered if I had an extra set. I thought I did and said I would call Adam right away to make arrangements to help him out. I called him at the Wings, Inc. office at St. Paul's Holman Field.

The St. Paul Downtown Airport, also known as Holman Field, is an airport just across the Mississippi River from downtown Saint Paul, Minnesota. The airport has three runways and serves a few large corporations in the local area, a flight training school and the Minnesota Army National Guard aviation unit, as well as transient general aviation aircraft.

"Wings Incorporated, Adam speaking."

"Hi Trippy. Mom called and told me you lost your truck keys. I think I might have a copy. How about I take you to lunch near your apartment and we can try my key."

Since his schedule was loaded that day (due to the awesome weather) he was more than pleased to get the help. I was eager to give it… anytime. This was my son, and I was immensely proud of who he had become as a man. I would have done anything for him. So, I made arrangements to meet him at the airport at about 11:30 that morning and from there it was a short ride to his apartment.

When I arrived at the airport, I noticed a Cessna 172 flying just above. As a pilot myself, I recognized it to be in the landing pattern, and possibly coming in for a landing on runway 31 or 32 at St. Paul's Holman Field. *"Perhaps it's Adam,"* I thought to myself. I watched with delight and hoped that the landing would be a *squeaker* for whom ever it was on board, likely a student pilot like myself.

I continued to watch as the plane banked left in the pattern to enter the downwind leg of the landing sequence. As I watched, the airplane suddenly broke free from its downwind leg and dropped to make a sudden landing on runway 8. I recognized it to be an emergency landing procedure and my suspicions of a student being on board were confirmed moments later.

Sure enough, Adam emerged from the cockpit along with a beaming student. He made Adam very happy with his performance. Adam had set him up with a *simulated engine out on landing* procedure. He was delighted with the student's performance. And, the landing was a squeaker too. "Hey Dad, how's it going? I'll be right with ya."

I waited for him to process his student and finalize the lesson before we took off for his apartment. On the way, he recalled how he had been pushing his student that day and that he was doing an excellent job. "I see you pulled an emergency landing procedure on him." I said. "Yea, he's really doing a great job and I think he'll be ready for his solo soon." he replied. Adam was proud of him. I knew what that meant too, since Adam was my flight instructor as well.

We drove on to his apartment and tried the key I had for his truck. It didn't work. I suggested that he call the dealer and ask for a new key to be made, that I would take care of the details later for him. I wanted to do anything I could to help him not have to deal with a mundane little thing like keys. He was working so hard at being the best he could be, in addition to working at being a new husband. I wanted to help relieve some of his stress, to help him in any way I could. I was extremely proud of him. I AM proud of him, still.

Since we couldn't get the truck going, I suggested we stop off for a bite of lunch on the way back to the airport. As usual, Adam insisted that it was not necessary to buy him lunch. Part of him was too proud to admit that being a flight instructor doesn't afford one the pleasures of eating out much, since they only get paid for actually spending time in the sky. Two dollars to Adam back then was gasoline for the truck for a week. Suffice it to say, he and his new wife, Karin, were not living the life of the rich and famous.

Karin was also at work that day, at a small medical office not far from their home. Although Karin's job was full-time and had benefits, she and Adam were no different than others their age, in that they struggled to make ends meet at the end of the month. They often found themselves stretching pasta meals into the next day's lunch. They both worked very hard and had wonderfully huge plans for their future. For example, Karin's goal was to be a stay-at-home mom just like Adam's mom had been. She wanted to raise babies and be a homemaker. It was her dream... a dream she would never realize with Adam.

We stopped for a double-cheese burger and fries with a large coke. To Adam, that was a meal. Well, at least during the day. Nothing could match the brilliance of his mom's cooking. He devoured everything she could invent in the kitchen. To Adam, her cooking was unmatched.

As we ate, we talked about my flight training progress and what the future was to hold for me as a pilot. Adam was always trying to encourage his students whenever he had a chance, and I was no exception. I mentioned to Adam that I felt I had made a fool of myself at the flight school, when I was scheduled to fly my last cross-country flight.

The schedule had gotten fouled up, and I had been rescheduled for a later time that day, without being notified. I had arrived early at 7am to make a four-hour flight. Now I was being told that I couldn't have a plane until 2pm that day. I was furious! I'm ashamed to say that I became loud and abusive with the dispatcher. I was not happy and let him know it. Rather rudely, I might add. The dispatcher would not budge. When I took the issue to Adam that Saturday morning he just said, "Everything is going to work out just fine, Dad." I left in a huff. I felt awful.

"Why am I acting this way? This isn't like me. What's going on with me?" I thought.

As I recalled the whole event to Adam, he said he remembered the details of what happened. I felt terrible that I embarrassed him at work. I looked him in the eye and asked for his forgiveness. It came immediately.

"Dad, forget it. You are forgiven. Say nothing more about it. It is forgotten. Just forget it Dad - it happens to all of us."

1:00 pm

I dropped Adam off at the airport and noticed his next student had just arrived. He was standing outside the gate of the flight school when we drove up.

"There's my next student, Adam said, *"Right on time. I like that."* He thanked me for lunch and for my help. And, as he left the car he gave me his usual handshake, the kind that starts out normal and ends up in five different positions with a snap of the fingers at the end. We both did it. It was OUR handshake, our bond. I felt so close to him.

The love for my son was and is immeasurable. When I think of how much I love my son and think of how much God loves me, I shudder. Adam was the perfect son, and more… he was my best male friend in the entire world. We were not only father and son, we were best friends, buddies. As I watched him proceed with his student I beamed with delight. I was so very, very proud.

As he walked away, his arm over the shoulder of his next student, I shouted from the car that I would call him that evening to make arrangements for my next cross-country flight. He turned and smiled. With a poised confidence, he winked and gave me the "thumbs up" sign for his approval. He was so confident, so poised. He was everything I had hoped for in a son. He continued on through the gate with his student, and as I began to drive away slowly I just watched him with delight in my rearview mirror. I felt a peace come over me, a peace I hadn't felt for a very long time. It was a familiar sensation, this peace. I knew it to be of God, the *"peace that passes understanding,"* for I had experienced it in the Boundary Waters Wilderness as a young man.

Then, suddenly, as unannounced as a blast of heat from an open oven door, while looking in the mirror at Adam, I heard a dark, ominous voice in my car. It came at me with a sense of attack and pushed me back in my seat. With a hellish darkness it simply said,

"This is the last time you will ever see your son alive."

My heart raced. At first, I looked all around inside the car, convinced there was a person *in* the car with me. Finding no one, I checked the radio figuring it was a commercial for a scary movie or something like that. The radio was turned off.

The only other possible explanation for this ominous voice was that it was all in my head, in my mind. But, I could not begin to imagine why I would think a thing like that. It was completely foreign to me, frightening and evil. I was bewildered and a bit shaken, but I decided to dismiss it off as a random, uninvited thought.

"Where did THAT come from?" I thought. *"What's going on with me lately?"* I could feel the

tension and stress of the day before once again ooze into my mood. I was confused and tired and now frightened by what I had just heard. It was getting late and I needed to get back to work.

Back at the office I re-entered the work-a-day world of high stress and tension of customers demanding this, the boss asking for that, and all the high-wire stuff each day seemed to be bringing me at that time in my life. As I walked through the door to my office I felt a great sense of dread come upon me. I felt overwhelmed. I hated my job then. I felt unappreciated and overworked. The phone rang...I went back to work, hearing the echo of that ominous voice in the car.

"...last time you'll ever see your son alive..."

Not likely! I knew my son. I loved my son. I watched him grow into a man, a fine man. He was a man of integrity, poise, strength of spirit and body. Adam had far exceeded the image of the man I had envisioned of him. To me, Adam was invincible, indestructible. He had become my hero. *"...last time..."* was clearly out of the question in my mind, in my heart.

But, as I had watched Adam walk through that gate and on into the little building of the flight school, it truly would, in fact, be the very last image of my son alive that I would ever have. Hellish mayhem loomed on the horizon, just a few hours away.

3:15 pm

"New Richmond traffic, Duchess one-eight-niner-six-zero turning base for runway three-two. Any traffic in the area please advise, New Richmond."

Just then, all hell broke loose. Far from my knowledge, as Adam flew his routine flying lesson, on a perfect flying day, the unimaginable happened.

For no understandable reason, in a fluke of engine failure, Adam's airplane began falling from the sky, stalling and turning away from the airport and into the town of New Richmond, Wisconsin. Adam was struggling with his very life, and the life of his student Jason.

Using all of the aviation knowledge, experience and expertise he possessed, Adam skillfully piloted his crippled plane to the ground. As the plane lost power, it forced a landing in the city, where after clipping a tall pine tree and breaking through power lines, Adam's twin-engine aircraft, the Duchess, emergency landed, wheels up, on the street of a small residential neighborhood.

Striking a small tree on the boulevard and tearing off the right wing, the aircraft's fuel sprayed and spilled onto the scene, bursting the airplane, my son, and his student, into flames.

Adam had quickly made his exit of the aircraft expecting Jason to follow close behind. Using all fours, Adam was seen scampering away from his burning aircraft, himself on fire. Blinded by the light and intensity of the flames, Adam found himself tangled up in a small pine tree in the yard where he was attempting his escape from the wreckage. Jason had been rendered unconscious in the right seat of the aircraft, where he died from the fire.

A neighbor, adjacent to the scene of the accident, was rushing to Adam's aid when he heard the thunderous explosion. With flames engulfing the aircraft and everything around it, including Adam, the man was unable to help. But he did hear Adam's last words…

"Jesus Save Me… Jesus Save Me."

Being trapped by the small tree engulfed by fire, Adam's soul followed Jesus into Heaven. Adam had died. And, I didn't know, I wouldn't know until hours later.

At 3:15 pm that day, I was completely unaware of the mayhem that was ensuing. I was in a meeting with a customer listening to the usual complaints of our company not having performed 100% all the time, missing a few orders, employee difficulties... blah, blah, blah. Little did I know that at that very moment my son, my precious Adam, was struggling with the final fight of his life, one that he would lose.

The meeting had droned on, *ad nauseum*, and by the end of the day I would find myself once again becoming saturated with anger and frustration and a growing sense of hopelessness. This and the course of my life leading up to that moment were smothering me. Life just seemed to be crashing in all around me and I didn't know why. I was exhausted emotionally and depleted by all the effort of trying to always do better. I guess I just felt like a failure, at least I did that day. Again, I was feeling spiritually under attack. I hated feeling like this.

5:15 pm

As I was in my car driving home, I found myself slipping back into self-pity and resentment for the foul condition of my life. I was a wreck emotionally; going from peaceful one minute to enraged the next, over some trivial, insignificant issue. People who knew me would not have described me that way. They would have said I was a model of organization, a pillar of emotional strength, someone others go to for help and guidance. Clearly, there were forces beyond any strength I possessed that relentlessly blew me off my true course. There I was, steeped in myself again, feeling trapped in something I could not understand, certainly could not share with anyone. I felt alone... again.

In an attitude of defiance, I began blaming God for all the rottenness in my life and the overwhelming pain I was feeling. I began charging Him with not coming through like He said He would in His Word. I began claiming that He was less than who He claimed to be.

My tirade went on for about five minutes when it stopped abruptly, when I heard from God... right there, in my car. His voice seemed both in my head and coming from inside the car at the same time, not unlike my previous experience at the airport that afternoon, however this voice was not dark. It was strong with a kindness in the tone. As I rounded the entrance ramp onto interstate I-694, I heard God speak to me...

"Mark, please, I don't want you to do that."

I responded harshly, filled with anger and self-pity, *"Oh, YOU don't want me to. Big deal! You don't want me to do anything do you? I always have to* be perfect, don't I? At work, at home, at church… well, not today!"

I could feel my blood pressure rising, my anger boiling within me. I was having the biggest emotional meltdown of my life and I didn't know why. The Lord responded in a louder and more serious tone…

"Mark, I'm asking you to not behave this way."

Again I responded with arrogance and disrespect towards God, *"How are you going to stop me? What will you do, kill my son?"* Then, a third time the Lord spoke to me. But this time His tone was more forceful, strict, authoritative and commanding…

"Mark, you don't understand. I'm telling you that I do NOT want you behaving this way."

By now my ego was in full swing, fueled by my anxiety, frustration, self-pity, and influenced by dark forces in my life, I foolishly responded with arrogance and anger toward God. My response was deliberate and direct. And I repeated those horrible words that would haunt me to this day, *"What will you do God, kill my son because I am not going to do what You want me to do?"*

Who was I kidding; I was feeding my desire to escape the trials and troubles of regular life with sinful behavior. I was lying to myself and now had challenged the position of God's authority with those spiteful words... words I choked on when I spoke them.

Immediately, there was silence in the car. I heard no more from the Lord regarding the issue. I drove on, forgetting what I had heard in the car earlier that day at the airport, ignoring my blatant disregard toward God's sovereignty, sinking in my troubles. I finally had my meltdown and was now completely spent emotionally.

5:30 pm

I arrived home from work and found Linda outside grilling ribs for dinner. It was actually a beautiful warm sunny day, although my mood made it feel like it was overcast and dreary. I tried to brush my troubles aside and not bring them into her world. I greeted her with a kiss on the cheek, like always, and asked how her day was. She seemed quite unnerved and tense, ignoring my interest in her.

She immediately asked me if I had heard of an airplane crash that day. I said no. They had become so frequent that summer that another just seemed normal news. The local TV stations had been inundated with aircraft accidents that summer. The most recent was one on White Bear Lake, not far from our home. It had been an elderly woman with her handicapped son, making a pleasure flight over the lake, buzzing neighbors and friends. While in low, slow flight, she lost control of her Mooney airplane when she suffered a stroke. The aircraft crashed into the waters off shore from the very friends she had been waving her wings to.

Linda said that another airplane had gone down, this time in New Richmond, Wisconsin. She asked if Adam ever flew to the town of New Richmond. I said yes, but did not know how often. I went inside and turned on the television to check out the news reports to see what I could learn. The scene was awful. On the side yard of a badly burned house laid the tangled, melted remains of a small airplane, and one body covered with a blanket. The plane was so badly destroyed it was difficult to identify it. The news reporters kept talking about a "single engine" and only "one pilot".

Immediately, I called the flight school and asked if Adam was out flying. "Yes," came the reply. I tensed up. Then I asked if he was alone. "No, he has a student with him." They replied. "What is he flying right now?" I asked. They told me he was with a student in the Duchess, a twin-engine aircraft.

65

I felt some relief since the news stations kept reporting of a single-engine plane crash. However, that relief was short lived.

Eventually, the news updates would give further details of a twin-engine "T" tail aircraft that belonged to Wings, Inc. out of the St. Paul downtown airport. A sense of panic began to creep in. *"The Duchess has a 'T' tail,"* I thought. I was beginning to feel uncertain and afraid, really afraid. Then I heard them say, *"Duchess"* and *"a second body was found in the wreckage."* I called the Wings office again, hoping Adam would answer and reassure me he was safe.

Call after call they would not confirm Adam's whereabouts. They only told me that he was overdue from a training flight with a student. The news folks had not yet discovered the identities of the pilots and we were beginning to suspect it could be them. We just didn't know. Finally, in a fit of fearful rage, I demanded that they tell me what was going on. Adam was now over two hours late, with no explanation from Wings as to why. They knew why… that twin engine Duchess aircraft was Wing's plane and Adam was the pilot. Adam and his student were dead!

One of the more seasoned instructors intercepted my last call, after my demands to the dispatcher. He got on the line and calmly stated something like…*"Mr. Triplett, we believe that you may have lost your son today. That is all I can tell you at this point. We just don't know any more than that. Adam was in the Duchess with a student and has not returned. He is two hours late."*

At that second I felt a powerful presence come over me and heard a gentle voice in my mind, *"this will not dismantle us."* I had absolutely no idea what that meant or where it came from. I dismissed it as another random thought. I asked the instructor on the phone if Adam had possibly changed flights, perhaps he took a plane up to Brainerd, MN (a repair facility), or perhaps he was signed out on the wrong airplane. I was desperate to find anything that could dispel the chilling statement *"…we believe you may have lost your son today."* It was not to be.

With each broadcast we learned more of the gruesome details of the accident, each one scanning more of the wreckage confirming what the Wings instructor had told me. *"Dear God, that's Adam's airplane,"* I thought to myself. *"That is my son under that blanket."* I withheld as much of my fear as I could get away with to protect my wife. I felt the weight of the world on my shoulders, felt the crushing weight of terror and sorrow falling down on top of our wonderful little family. I had completely forgotten all about my wretched conversation with God earlier that evening, but it would eventually find its way back into my consciousness, to taunt and condemn me.

We began calling family, neighbors, church friends... anyone who knew us. Adam's sister Katrina, then four months pregnant with her first child, came immediately. I called Karin, Adam's wife of only three months. She arrived later with her parents. I ached inside for them both as their tears flowed and their bodies shook with tension and fear.

Soon, our little house was filled, each room to capacity, with loving friends and family. Everyone was crying. We all waited to hear more, more confirmation, *if* it really was Adam or not. We hoped we were wrong, that the reporters had erred and that Adam would call or come walking through the front door wondering what all the commotion was about. He never came. The county sheriff did. And with him, he brought a Police Chaplain.

Having been in law enforcement for a few years I knew why they came. They asked for permission to obtain the dental records of Adam, that they presumed he was killed in the accident, but could not confirm it. The bodies of the two pilots were burned beyond human recognition. Almost 11 hours later they returned to confirm Adam's death. Katrina screamed and ran out of the house. Karin slumped into her parent's arms and sobbed. Linda and I held each other and shook with an enormity of fear, emptiness, and grief. That was the day we entered the Valley of the Shadow of Death.

The next night our neighbors placed 500 luminaries along our street, representing a runway for Adam to find his way home. It led right up to our front door. The second night they added 500 more, and 500 more on the third night, until there were 1500 luminaries lining our street. The local TV news crew filmed that loving dedication by our neighbors, commenting that it was something they had never witnessed before. A friend and fellow pilot flew over the scene on the last evening and told us that it could be seen from high in the sky. Other pilots too, filled the skies above our house. Each hour, it seemed, an airplane circled the house and waved its wings in a memorial salute to Adam and his family. This went on for days.

The visitation at the funeral home was filled to capacity, causing traffic jams and extremely long lines. People were crammed into the building and out the door, with lines leading off into the parking lot and onto the sidewalks. Everyone who came patiently waited. The funeral home director stopped counting visitors at 650, saying that it was impossible to keep track of so many people. What an honor to have so many present, to pay their respects.

I remember greeting each and every person that came. At one point I looked up and I saw a sea of human beings. There were so many of Adam's friends and family, Linda's co-workers as well as mine, all crowded into that place. It was difficult to recognize them until it became their time to visit me next to the casket. So many came!   What an honor they bestowed.

Adam's elementary school bus driver was there. His day-care teacher when he was four years old came. His friends from school, church folks, co-workers and bosses he worked with, they all came. People from near and far: Minnesota, Arizona, Washington, California, North Carolina, people kept coming.   Family, friends, neighbors, church members, even people I considered to be my enemies… they came too! It was overwhelming. It was honoring. It was pure love.

The next day the funeral was held at Wildwood Church. The building was filled to overflowing, with many people were standing out in the garden area adjacent to the sanctuary while others were crammed into the halls and entryways. Some just stood outside in the parking lot, listening to the service through the open doors. There was not an empty seat anywhere in the church.

A month earlier, Adam had commented to the church membership that somehow, some way, he was going to fill the church to capacity. He had become a bit dismayed at the poor attendance of our annual meeting when only 28 people showed up. With the enthusiasm of being a recent Moody Bible Institute student, and now the Youth Leader of Wildwood Church, he was rightfully concerned about the poor attendance when he said it was, "*the most important day in the year for the organization of this church body.*" Little did anyone realize at that time just how true his statement would be. He had fulfilled his promise to "*...fill this place to capacity.*" Sadly that day, Wildwood Church was indeed overflowing, however filled with honor for this young man of God.

In the months following his funeral, I came to remember that awful conversation I had with God the day Adam died. I struggled with the thought that I had possibly caused all the horror that my family now faced. I couldn't sleep. I couldn't eat. I couldn't function at all. Finally, after two months, I went to my wife to confess to her how I had acted that day and that I was afraid I might be to blame for Adam's death.

She listened with heightened intensity. When I finished there was a long pause of silence. I stood there naked in my vulnerability to her response, whatever that would be. I was afraid that I was about to lose my wife, my life with her, and the potential of any remnant of sanity in my life at all. But I was determined to have all truth revealed to me and even about me. I could hear my heart beating in my chest. I waited an eternity for her response.

Finally she walked over to me, and with tears in her eyes she embraced me and said *"Mark, it's not your fault."* She then pointed out that when I had stated those foolish words to the Lord that it was 5:15pm, two hours *after* Adam had died. What gracious love she demonstrated that day.

I was grateful for her not throwing me out of the house, abandoning me in my true "hour of need", but I felt I was dying inside. I would continue to struggle with the question of whether God had taken my son from me for something I had done. Clearly, a person suffering the death of a child does not have the fullness of reasonable, comprehensive thoughts as before experiencing the loss. There are so many explosive emotions going on all at once. It's like trying to listen to a whisper while standing in the middle of rush-hour traffic racing all around you. I could not "reason it out" in my own mind, so I sought the wise counsel of other Christian leaders.

In my search for the truth and answers to my dilemma, I wrote to Joyce Meyer, Dr. Billy Graham, Dr. James Dobson, Dr. Ravi Zacharias, and many others too. The work of these fine, godly people was the salve of God's love that never fails. It began the healing work in my sore and wounded life. They all took the time, in one way or another, to reassure me that our loving heavenly Father, our Lord and Savior, our Creator and compassionate caregiver just simply does NOT operate in a way of vindictive, jealous rage and dictatorial judgment. In short, they all affirmed that God is NOT in the business of killing our children to punish us or to get our attention, or even to serve a future calling.

Rather, what I've discovered in the time since Adam's death is that God works much differently than that. Go with me, back to the wretched conversation I had with God the day Adam died. My conversation was at 5:15 p.m. Adam died at 3:15 p.m. So, did God "jump ahead" two hours in time to see if I would sin against Him bad enough to "kill my son?" If so, why not jump ahead two years... ten years... twenty-three years? If my sin against Him was going to be so great in 1997, why not just destroy Adam at age two instead? Why give him to me at all?

In fact, in 1976, at age two Adam mistakenly drank a small amount of insecticide one summer day, thinking it was a cool glass of water. With Adam choking and turning blue, I raced to the emergency room of the local hospital in St. Paul, and

I prayed... *"Dear God in Heaven, please save my son... please, dear God."* Adam was spared with no ill effects.

So, does it make any sense that our loving, and caring heavenly Father could see any distance into the future, would it not seem more merciful to take Adam at two instead of twenty-three, in light of my sin? This is where the devil wants us to believe that God is the source of our pain and suffering. Dr. Ravi Zacharias most clearly, and understandably unravels this perplexing mystery in his book titled, *Jesus Among Other_Gods.* He also visits the issue of pain and suffering in his other writings. Adam considered him one of the finest Christian thinkers of our time. I believe he was right.

Shortly after my conversation with Linda, we began professional counseling. For two-and-one-half years we were counseled back to a sense of reason and healing within. We are forever grateful to God for His gift of love through the dedication and loving care of Dr. Marcus Bachmann. Week after week, month after month he helped us struggle with our pain, loss, fear and confusion. He also helped us understand, from a Christian perspective, how to carry on in our loss. After every session with us he prayed for us. Our doctor prayed!

I will never say that we are all better now, or that life has been restored back to normal because it will never happen – ever. However, I've learned that life can be lived with the pain and suffering the death of a child brings. Holidays are still somewhat empty events, hollow joy without Adam's presence. Guilt stabs us constantly too. The loss we feel with Adam not being here robs us of the pleasure of enjoying our beautiful daughter Katrina and her family. That's the way mayhem operates. It steals, kills and destroys.

Today, when I look back on the landscape of my life, I see the hand of God everywhere. I see Him in the diligence of my parents who spared themselves luxuries for my benefit. I see the grace of God in presenting me with opportunities to learn and grow and enjoy his creation. I see His generosity in presenting me with the gift of a lifetime in my wife, whom I met at the ripe age of 15 and as of this writing have been married to for over forty-one years. I see his faithfulness in his ever-present help when people and circumstances foiled my attempts at success or happiness. No matter what or where, I see His love – the love that never fails. His love is quiet, often invisible and always present. God's love is pure. That perspective would be tested to the very limits of my ability to think, feel or even believe in Him any longer, as the mayhem of my son's death would tear at my soul.

When it comes to the faithfulness of God to keep His word regarding *"I will never leave you nor forsake you,"* I guess you could say that God's love is like a snowplow that clears the way for us, or it is the tow-truck that rescues us from the ditch of our mistakes and misfortunes. Either way, He will be there for us, no matter what we decide to do with our lives, right or wrong. It would take years for me to be able to see the truth of God's presence and care in my life, long after the death of my son.

In the early years after Adam's death, as I struggled to unwrap the mystery of it, God showed up in miraculous ways giving answers to my pleas as I begged Him to help me make sense of the mayhem in my life. He showed up in spades… producing real miracles in my life, miracles that would change the course of my life and of my faith.

Yes… God still performs miracles, even today, in the 21st century. The chapter, *Miracles,* is a true account of the miraculous events of my life in the months after Adam died. Pleading with the Lord to help me unravel the twisted, disjointed things I was feeling and thinking, I was presented with answers in the form of miracles. But first I would have to face My Grief… alone.

CHAPTER FOUR

My Grief

The Villain

I was walking past the refrigerator in the kitchen when it happened... the grief wave... *My Grief*. It was the first time I had experienced such intense sorrow and cutting sadness since the death of my son. My state of shock and just trying to hold up and *be strong* under the strain from the death of my son helped to keep My Grief at bay for a while. Oh, I did a fair amount of crying in the days between Adam's death and his funeral. I cried a lot. But it was nothing like what I was about to experience. I was alone in the house when it arrived... unannounced, like a thief.

I had gone to the kitchen to get something to drink and I paused to look at the photos Linda had so neatly arranged on the door of our refrigerator... pictures of our children... pictures of Adam. I melted into each one, traveling back to the time each photo was taken, a time of life, happiness and joy. As I ran my fingers over the face of my little boy in one photo and onto the next as a young man I became overwhelmed with a deluge of emotions and crumbled under the weight of it all. I collapsed onto the kitchen floor, sobbing so deeply I could not breathe, choking on my own sorrow.

It was there, on the kitchen floor where I finally met My Grief face-to-face. It wasn't the grief of others in the family, the grief and sorrow I was trying my best to fend off of those I loved. It wasn't the grief that stabbed at the heart of our neighborhood that mourned the loss of our dear, Adam. This was My Grief. He had finally arrived to inflict on me the most devastating sorrow and sadness the human heart can bear. His attack was swift and accurate, like a samurai slicing clean through my soul to split me in two.

This grief, My Grief, was relentless and untiring in his pursuit of my sanity and peace. Feeding on my very being he continued to charge and wage war within me. Only when I became nearly unconscious from the breathless weeping did he relent… for only a short while. I crawled into the family room and fell, limp onto the couch where the life force within me drained outward into the quiet room, a silence broken only by my moans and deep sobbing.

My defenses were completely gone. I was alone in My Grief now, weakened by the strain of trying to keep my composure, to *stay strong* for the others. Now I had to face him, one-on-one. I tried to stand up, to *take my stand* and regain my strength. Nothing. My legs would not hold me up. There I lay, a prisoner of My Grief. I cried until my eyes burned and my sides ached from the deep thrusting sobs that seemed to come from a place within me that I had never met. I was limp in my sorrow, unable to fend for myself, as My Grief would retreat and advance in wave after wave.

I must have passed out, or fallen asleep on the couch because I was wakened by Linda coming in the back door. I pulled myself together, wiped my eyes and made my way to the kitchen, that recent battlefield of my emotional self and My Grief. Linda needed help bringing in bags of groceries or something, not sure what I was carrying. I think she was talking to me... I think I was answering her. Not sure. I was in a fog. I went into the bathroom to wash my face and try to regain my composure.

Splashing cold water repeatedly on my face felt good, like I was closing up a wound and reducing the swelling around my eyes. The coolness of the water made me forget the searing heat from my tears that had flowed unstopped for hours that morning. The cool water on my face gave me some temporary relief. As I dried my face in the towel I could feel the soft fibers moving across my face, scratching the now cracked corners of my bloodshot eyes and raw nose. I switched from rubbing to dabbing softly. Covering my entire face I pressed inward to gently absorb the water from it while attempting to smother any remnant of My Grief's attempt to scar me further. I finally gave out a final moan, deep into the towel as I finished my chore.

Setting the towel down I slowly raised my eyes to look in the mirror, to assess my attempt at trying to wipe away my tears. I stared myself down, looking at a stranger in the mirror. This man, worn and ragged was not me, not the forty-something man I knew. This was a victim of a beating, a man drained of himself. I wondered who I had just become.

I stared at the man in the mirror and there was something deep within me that wanted to fight back, to deny the enemy any victory over MY life. I challenged the man in the mirror and promised to "...never quit, never give in, never give up...keep fighting." I didn't know what I was in for, this battle with My Grief. How could I know? This was a part of myself that had never been revealed, never let loose, never freed to inflict pain and hurt this deep. But on that day we met, and I was determined that he would not win over me.

I returned to the kitchen to continue helping Linda put away groceries, each time glancing at the pictures on the refrigerator, feeling the swelling of sorrow and loss rising up within me, as My Grief taunted me from the sidelines. I counter-punched with reading the labels on the food, checking the prices of each item, anything to keep him at bay. It worked... for now, but not for long.

What I didn't realize at the time was that My Grief was regrouping as well, calling on reinforcements of his own, reinforcements like fear, anger, frustration, worry, shame and a host of other warriors in the battle for my sanity. I would soon learn that the battle had only just begun and would continue for a very long time. It wasn't long after that episode there on the kitchen floor that Linda and I began professional counseling with Dr. Marcus Bachmann where we would strategize and analyze the tactics of My Grief... and Linda's.

My mind began twisting me in ways I was not used to, antagonized by My Grief and his desire to destroy. My Grief quickly employed the tactic of confusion. I was becoming forgetful, not remembering to do things Linda had asked me to do just moments before. I simply did not remember her asking me. I would take things out into the garden as if I were beginning a new project and then just stare at it, wondering what the original idea could have been to warrant such an arsenal of tools. There were times I would find myself staring into the refrigerator wondering what I was looking for, or questioning if I was even hungry. Dazed, I would suddenly discover myself walking through the grocery store pushing a cart through the aisles wondering how I got there and what I was shopping for. My Grief was gaining ground in my battle for sanity.

Sensations or physical symptoms of My Grief continued to show up, and in number. I experienced loss of appetite. I found myself struggling with sleeplessness, waking very early in the morning (like 3 or 4 am). I constantly had a knot in the pit of the stomach and a burning and tightness in my throat. I was prone to sighing to catch my breath, often disguising it with a yawn or two. I was constantly tired and felt chest pain or tightness that felt as if someone was literally squeezing my heart with a huge fist.

I had difficulty swallowing and felt weak most of the time. Diarrhea was my constant companion in the first few months, but faded as my appetite came back to life. I began to eat more fiber and raw foods like vegetables and fruits. Suffering already with tinnitus, that incessant ringing in my ears, I noticed that it too had become louder and more irritating, often waking me in the middle of the night. Overall, my physical body was manifesting outward signs of my inward warfare. It was enough to drive me insane! I decided I needed to make a visit to my doctor's office.

My doctor suggested I start myself on Zoloft, or some such medication, just to take the edge off. I refused, stating I was going to *stay awake* to the things happening in my life no matter how painful or frightening. Besides, if I had taken any of those mood-enhancing type drugs my flying privileges would be revoked. I would NOT let anything get in the way of me holding on to the one thing Adam and I shared so deeply.

No, I would stay awake through this storm no matter what. I agreed to slow down on the coffee and started eating more healthy foods, and regularly. It gave me a great deal of relief. In fact, switching to a decaffeinated green tea seemed to be a much better choice of drink than coffee, even the decaffeinated type. I was still fighting all the symptoms, but didn't feel so immobilized by them as before. I made the conscious decision to put my flying on hold for a while to allow my body and mind to regain a sense of strength and unity. It was then that I decided to return to work.

A few weeks after returning to work, I discovered yet another characteristic of My Grief. It was very odd, this thing called My Grief, who seemed to be focused on my destruction. It had My Name associated with it. How can that be?!? Was there something inside ME that wanted to die? I soon discovered the answer to that question is as old as human suffering itself. The answer is almost always a resounding yes. The response is, at first, always try to fight back, which I was most certainly doing, constantly. But I felt as if I was losing that battle and my will to survive dwindling. Sometimes we lose the fight and the results are devastating to all those left behind to mourn. I was determined to NOT be a casualty of this new war. I would fight to the bitter end if need be, but I would fight back. Suicide was simply NOT an option.

Each day, as I drove in rush hour traffic I had time to reflect on the events that brought me to this horrid place in my life. Each day, I would try to unravel the mystery of it all. Each day, I would pray, continually, without ceasing, searching for answers. As the days progressed into weeks I found myself diminished in my abilities to function at the same level as before the accident. I grew increasingly frustrated with drivers on the road, seemingly unaware of my broken life as they cut me off in traffic, nearly ran me off the road at intersections and in general looked as if they too wanted me dead. I became cautious of everyone around me, especially those in motor vehicles.

I tried to function normally back at the office, not letting My Grief interfere with my work. I couldn't see how he was affecting me, or my emotions especially when someone would ask about "how are you doing?" I guess I must have emoted more than they expected, making them all feel a bit uncomfortable. Poor souls... feeling a bit, *uncomfortable* with My Grief. It didn't take long before I was called into the boss's office.

He proceeded to tell me that I needed to get back to the level of my former self, to suck it up and to *"grieve on [my own] time, after five pm,"* that he had *"a business to run,"* and needed me *"working at full capacity."* He continued to tell me that he "understood" my pain, but that I needed to get back to 100%. I left his office crushed. How could he possibly *understand* my pain, My Grief?!?

I was profoundly hurt and confused. I wondered if I had done something wrong, made a costly mistake for the company or offended a customer. I wondered if everyone in the office felt the same way. I felt completely alone... abandoned by all those I trusted to help carry me through this battle with My Grief.

As hard as I tried, I was unable to cope with the added pressure to *"get back to 100%"* so I contacted the division office of our Human Resources Department in Colorado. I told my story to the person who answered the phone and was immediately transferred to a director within the organization. Calmly, she asked me to tell my story, to take all the time needed to explain my call that day. I told her my son had recently died in a fiery airplane accident, just three weeks before, that I was attempting to return to work, but evidently was not working at a satisfactory level, that my boss was pressuring me to work harder or I may find myself looking elsewhere for a job.

She asked me to stop, told me she had heard enough, that WE would all be on a conference call together first thing the next morning (as my boss had already left for the day), and that I was not to worry about my job or my position within the company. She very sincerely stated how awful it must be for me and my family to have suffered such a terrible loss and that she would do whatever she could to help me in this current crisis. She told me to just go home and care for my wife and daughter, for now.

The next morning I arrived as usual, albeit a bit nervous about the upcoming conference call. The boss seemed a bit nervous as well and closed his door as I passed by. I wondered what was about to happen. I was in no frame of mind to sort anything out, let alone corporate policy and such. I was fighting a daily battle with My Grief. I could barely remember where I parked my car each day, or to wear a belt or check to see if I had two different shoes on my feet. The phone rang. It was from Colorado. My heart raced and my mouth became dry as I answered the phone. Within minutes she had added my boss to the call and stated that it would be very wise of him to simply be silent during the call, that she would be doing all the talking. "Mark... are you here, on the call with us?" "Yes." I replied somewhat sheepishly. My heart pounded in my chest.

She proceeded to tell my boss that I would be taking the next three months off from work, with her personal approval, as a medical leave of absence to work out the sufferings of our immense loss. *"Further..."* she went on to alert the boss that my job would not be in jeopardy, that my position with the company and with this account would be safe and intact upon my return.

Her orders were firm and unyielding to him. When asked if he understood, his only words during the entire call were *"I do."* I could tell by his tone that this was not over, not yet. She told me to go home, to take two to three months to get through this very hard time, to seek professional help and to take care of myself, and my family, that they were my first priority. I left immediately, thanking God for her and what she had just done for me.

All the way home I remained in a stunned state. No one had ever stood up for me like she did, not ever. A calm came over me and for the first time since I heard those dreadful words from the Wings Inc. dispatcher, *"...Mr. Triplett, we believe you may have lost your son today."* It was a calm that gave me the sense that perhaps I was not alone in my battle with this villain, My Grief.

I never really got the chance to thank her for what she did for me, as she had moved on in the company shortly after and I lost track of her by the time I returned to the office. However, I will always be grateful for what she did that day. She, in her compassion and positional power gave me the time and space needed to find the hope to survive this most horrid of life's trials.

Weeks turned into months and soon it would be time for me to return to work, as arranged. I was feeling a bit stronger, clearer in my mind and the battles with My Grief had been waged and seemingly won, for now. Nervously, I made the call to inform my boss of my plans to return to the office, to return to my job. His response was abrupt and cold. Life back at the office seemed normal, for the most part. I made quick adjustments and fell into my normal routine. I struggled at first, but I made progress. Decision-making was difficult. I was still grappling with this adversary within me, My Grief.

He was back and in full force. Actually, he never really left me. He would retreat temporarily from his onslaught, only to return in full force and make attempt after attempt to inflict his harm. No matter where or when, I would find the urgent need, whether at the office or at home, to excuse myself to go and walk off stress or sit quietly in my car in an attempt to break the relentlessness of his attacks. Prayer was constant.

For lunch I would drive a few miles down the road to a quiet spot, reflecting on God's Word and trying to apply it to my struggles. Each day I came away refreshed and renewed with a bit more strength, more stamina to face tomorrow. It was a very long, very difficult road to travel, this dark valley of death, and I was nowhere near the end, but I was making progress. Then the bottom fell out. The boss called me into the conference room, shut the door and proceeded to inform me that I was being transferred to the downtown office in Minneapolis. I screamed "NO!" Everyone in the office heard me. They all knew what was happening and no one could reveal it to me or do anything about it.

My world once again had collapsed. I was just starting to regain a sense of composure, a sense of healing (albeit very small) and stability with my new life. Now I was thrust into a strange world, with different people, people I did not know, work I was not familiar with, to a place I hated to work in. Nothing could be done. I was to be moved by week's end. I was completely broken. On the way home that evening I could feel the presence of My Grief gloating in victory of winning this battle. The energy in my body was draining and I was losing the fight. Worry consumed me and heartbreak blanketed me with a penetrating sense of betrayal from all my co-workers, people I had spent nearly a decade working with, giving my very best to. No one came to my rescue. No one dared cross swords with the boss.

I cried deeply that night, while trying to get to sleep. It felt like another death to me. My identity had been once again altered by the actions of something outside my power to control. I went to sleep that night feeling defeated, worn out and broken. Over the following few months at my new assignment I began to learn more of what precipitated the old boss's actions to remove me from my decade long, stable work environment to this new, uncharted territory, where most of the people around me didn't even know my name. What I discovered was that revenge and retaliation were his motive. To make matters worse, my income had been slashed down by the removal of the commission payments due for my work on that account that year.

I was placed into a new account where all the commissions had already been awarded. I was to lose 20% of my income overnight, with no hope of recovering my bonus pay or being compensated for the work I would be doing on the new account. My Grief fanned the flames of my sadness with anger and frustration. My Grief recanted these destructive facts to me daily of how much I had lost... my son, my stable work... my income... my friends, and it would continue. I began to pray even harder, more often. I cried out to the Lord daily.

While the intent of my former boss was one of retaliation for having challenged his authority with the Human Resources Director's involvement, his actions to inflict harm soon fell to the wayside. God's Word became alive in a very mighty way. My new boss, Lynda M. became an oasis in my desert of despair. She gave me plenty of work to keep me productive, but not so much as to overwhelm me. She cared for me in a very personal way, calling me "Buddy" often, and in the presence of co-workers. She would include me in breaks for coffee and casual chats in the conference room from time-to-time with others in the group. She fed my soul with kindness.

A few months later I discovered that Lynda had taken my financial dilemma to the higher-ups, made a case for me and was able to recoup some of my earning losses that my former boss had cleverly extracted from me in his attempt to punish me. I also learned that at the same time he had failed to produce well enough on the old account to where the bonus pay was reduced dramatically within his entire account. When I became aware of this news, a Bible verse quickly came to mind, " *You intended to harm me, but God intended it for good…*" Genesis 50:20 (NIV) Scripture was being lived out in real time and in my real life.

It wasn't long after, everyone in our department learned of a deadly cancer that had invaded the body of my former boss's daughter. She was only 18 years old and had less than a year to live. Almost immediately, he decided to quit his job, he no longer *"had a business to run."* I felt a deep sadness for him and for his entire family. I knew what they would now be faced with. Soon, His Grief would visit him, unannounced… like a thief.

I would work with my new boss, Lynda for nearly two years before I decided to take an early retirement. Leaving the company I had invested 30 years of my life was a decision not easily made, especially now with the new friendships I had made. My Grief was there, all the while taunting me with issues of doubting my decision or worries about my future. My Grief showed up at the oddest of places and times, like during hugs at my retirement party. There were times I began to doubt if I had made the right decision, to retire at age 49. But, I went for it. In a spirit of defiance to My Grief, I retired on April 1st, April Fool's Day of 2000. And I never looked back. My wife Linda and I had a new calling on our lives and it was time to move on, to "Press On," like the song by Selah encourages us to do.

Moving forward with what I can only describe as a new godly calling on our lives, Linda and I created LNF (Love Never Fails) Ministries and The Adam M. Triplett Memorial Scholarship Funds. It took nearly a full year to become registered with the state of Minnesota as a 501 c. 3. nonprofit organization. Along the way, My Grief (and Her Grief) continued the never-ending attacks. It seemed they were always ready to pounce when things didn't go as planned.

Setbacks are common in life and no different with me. I could handle setbacks well, being disciplined to always look at the big picture and to the future. But, this grief journey took me to dark places within me that at times prevented me from doing just that. Those were times of considerable trial. Even when we tried to celebrate the formation of LNF Ministries we were stopped and reminded that the only reason we were engaged with it in the first place was because Adam was dead. It was a bittersweet victory.

Holidays, anniversaries, special dates all would bring on a gradual swelling of tension and discomfort for us. My Grief was always there ready to inflict any harm he could muster. I would be taken aback by a song or a smell, reminding me of Adam and how much he loved life, how he loved his life with us.

Years after finally selling off his little green Ford Ranger, I became overwhelmed while driving the freeway one day as a truck just like Adam's passed me. The driver looked very much like Adam as he passed by. I remember gasping as if I were seeing a ghost of Adam driving beside me. I began to shake and lose focus of my place on the road. I pulled over to the side of the road for a while to process it, new tears streaming down my face.

Another time of unexpected grief wave occurred in the Boundary Waters while on a trip with men from our church. I had a long-standing love affair with the Boundary Waters Canoe Area Wilderness. As a young boy I had found the lure of the Boundary Waters early in life and the experience became an integral part of my soul. It was a time of my transition from boyhood to manhood. I had always wanted the opportunity, one day to bring my son to the Boundary Waters to experience its magic, to share with him the splendor of God's creation and the indescribable peace and serenity found there. It never happened. While on that trip, My Grief reminded me continually of my failure to expose him to this wondrous place, making me feel even more of a loss of his presence. That trip marked a departure for me. I've only been back twice since, with a much less meaningful experience. My Grief is indeed a thief!

It took me a while, but after a few years I began to notice a pattern in my response to the grief experience in my life and the lives of others around me. I decided to fight back with an old tactic myself – fight fire with fire. My Grief seemed bent on bringing me to my knees, weeping and crying over my losses, making me feel deep loss and regret all the time. He was there constantly to remind me of the names and places that brought tears to my eyes, often causing me to channel my feeling AT God, not TO Him. Inside me I knew that was wrong, simply the wrong method of enlisting the Almighty God to work on my behalf. So, I fought back the only way I knew how… I went to the cemetery to share it with Adam and God. But I had to get on my knees first.

I went to the cemetery often, to cry, to get on my knees before God and pray. Once I even put my very face down, in the dirt, and prayed. But this time it would be different. This time I would not be pleading or wailing. No… this time I would be praising God for what I had lost, praising Him for having a son named Adam in the first place, thanking Him for my wounded heart that confirmed my deep appreciation and love for my son. I thanked Him for my tears, testifying to the sincerity and loyalty of my love for my little boy, tears of joy over the sadness that saturated my soul with regret over his death.

If I would be spending the rest of my life in tears they would be tears of joyful expression, tears of gratitude for having so much love in my heart that my loss demanded I pour it out in tears. I struggled to get the very words off my lips and out of my mouth, but I did it. And with each expression flowed a river of tears, a flood from my soul.

I would praise God for giving me a heart of love, even this broken heart. I would welcome the tears as evidence that I had been loved, am still loved, and that I still could love. My tears are now evidence of my love, not sorrow or sadness. My Grief had been dealt a fatal blow, but he would return, wounded himself, but relentless in his pursuit and purpose.

Through the following years, the tactics of My Grief were employed over and over to the point that I began to recognize his advance early in my onset of sorrow and pain. There were times when, particularly during holidays and special dates that he would arrive at my door. Without warning a wave of deep sorrow and loss and pain and worry and regrets... a flood of emotional upheaval would be unleashed on me, rendering me moody and out of sorts for weeks before the actual day of importance.

Holidays were the worse. So much seasonal tradition and festivity is associated with the Thanksgiving and Christmas holidays for us. Adam LOVED the holidays, making special arrangements to always be with us. Each time, I would fight back with tears of gratitude and thanksgiving, and not the tears of loss and morning My Grief desired for me.

No matter how difficult it would feel, and it WAS difficult and sometimes I failed at it, I pressed on with my tactic of using my tears as evidence of love being present before, during and ever after Adam's death.

My Grief has remained with me all these years since Adam's death, continually making attempts to drive me down to the ground of despair. He is with me even today and I suspect he will be with me until the day I die. But I fight him. Always!

I've now learned to recognize many of his tactics over the years and have fought back, as I challenged and promised the man in the mirror so many years ago. This war continues to rage on, and I have accepted his relentless attacks as the new norm, facing each one with everything within me to survive. And, I will survive. More than that… I choose to live in the splendor of LOVE… bathed in my own tears if necessary, until the day I die… because I love my son and my son loves me, and I love my God and my God loves me, and the **miracle** of love is that Love Never Fails! (1Cor 13:8 NIV)

"Miracles… seem to me to rest not so much upon faces or voices or healing power coming suddenly near to us from afar off, but upon our perceptions being made finer, so that for a moment our eyes can see and our ears can hear what is there about us always."

~ Willa Cather

CHAPTER FIVE

Miracles

Evidence of God's Love

The very word miracle conjures up ideas and visions of mystical and magical events, inexplicable and mysterious. Jesus Christ performed some of the most notable miracles ever recorded. For instance, turning water into wine, walking on water, healing the blind, the sick, the lame, and many more. Then there are recorded accounts of others performing miracles like Moses as he parted the Red Sea to free the nation of Israel from the Egyptian army that had pursued them into the desert to slay them.

Many people believe strongly in miracles, while others do not believe in them at all. They believe in coincidence. But I think everyone agrees that there are times when events occur where there is no rational or sane explanation. Throughout history there have been countless occurrences of unexplained events, grand and mostly unbelievable;

99

accounts of people being rescued from a burning building or auto accident by a person that cannot be accounted for. I can personally attest to the fact, by way of multiple events in my life, particularly following the death of Adam and my struggle to grip the meaning and sense of it all, that miracles are in fact real events which occur with amazing regularity and with profound results.

I have come to reason in my own mind and heart that miracles are a form of expression from God, one of the ways He communicates with His creation. Miracles are like a language to Him, a language that can be understood if one looks, listens and learns. I believe God uses miracles to speak to our hearts and minds, to reveal His presence or to render an answer to perplexing questions we have about the meaning of things in this life and in the next.

I have asked myself, "Why does God perform miracles?" The answer, I believe, is that He does so to encourage us, give us direction, fulfillment of our purpose in life, to build our hope, restore our faith and ignite love in our lives. There are many times in our lives where we simply cannot explain how or even why something happens. We often call it "coincidence," for lack of a deeper understanding of the event. I've tried to listen to the language of it all, to understand God's voice in the miracle, to glean

His meaningful message for my life. I really DO believe in miracles!

In the following pages, I will share with you many experiences from my own life's struggles that I believe were miracles from God. I am only reporting what actually happened to me and to my family before and after Adam died. I am not trying to boast in myself because these miracles happened. Rather, if I boast, let me boast in the tenderness of God's never failing love and in His infinite abilities, not mine. He speaks... I listen, watch and learn. He reveals in His timing. I wait, wait, wait.

God chooses to communicate with His creation in His way, His timing, and for His purpose. As I hope to show you in this chapter, miracles not only demonstrate the power and presence of our heavenly Father, but they also bring messages of forgiveness, hope, reassurance, and sometimes even direct answers to our questions of Him. I believe that all of the miracles I've experienced and witnessed were given for a specific purpose. I believe they were to bring messages of truth, comfort, and revelation needed for specific situations at the time in my grief journey. But they are also delightful proclamations from a loving Father, the lover of our souls.

We all can be witnesses to God's loving miracles each and every day, in one way or another, but we often turn our "faith eyes" from them, and dismiss the beauty of God's love for us by trying to explain them away as coincidence, natural events or chance happening. I know differently, and it is my desire that by sharing these deeply personal experiences with you, God will open the door of your heart and mind to the reality that He still works real miracles today, even in the 21st century.

Here now are just a few of the miracles I've experienced… and may God be glorified in their telling.

Thanksgiving Eve Service – 1996

As the music director of Wildwood Church it was my great pleasure to direct the small, but very dedicated congregation in singing during all worship services. With only a piano and regular folks singing slightly out of tune, we made our "joyful noise unto the Lord" each Sunday.

Special church events were very intimate, often inspirational and always joyful, whether it was a Christmas Eve service, Easter or Thanksgiving. One particular event was the Thanksgiving Eve Service of 1996 when the supernatural took over and I experienced a most wonderful, frighteningly beautiful miracle. It would be many months before I could sort it all out, to bring any meaning to it. It was the Thanksgiving before Adam's death.

As usual, I was directing the congregation in singing praise and worship songs and even some favorite old hymns during that service. With only twenty or thirty people present that evening, we sang praises to our Lord, thanking Him for His blessings and provisions. At one point, while we were singing an old hymn of thanks, I motioned to the pianist to play softly while I offered the congregation words of encouragement as we sang.

I asked the congregation to continue singing this beautiful song of thanksgiving, while reflecting on everything we could think about that God had done for each of us recently. I asked for everyone to reverentially offer thanks to our God while we continued to sing.

As the piano played we closed our eyes and lifted our voices in thanksgiving and sang with sincerity and reverential praise in our hearts. It was beautiful. There was a difference in the music. It became more saturated with feeling and humility. As we sang I personally melted into the beauty of the oneness of our spirits flowing upward to our precious Lord and I remember feeling so very close to His presence just then.

As I drifted into the serenity of the moment, I became startled by what I can only describe as the most beautiful sound of a choir singing just behind me, up on the platform. Their voices were a collection of perfectly harmonized vocals that seemed to paint colors of sound and had scales that seemed to have almost a three-dimensional characteristic.

Their beauty was awesome, wonderful, and beyond human description. I quickly turned around to see who was singing behind me with such splendor, color, and intense depth. There was no one there! And as quickly as I turned to look, the voices faded away and all I could hear was our little congregation singing, slightly out of tune.

I experienced intense feelings of fulfillment and loss all at the same time. I lost my place, and I recall that I needed to catch up with the congregation. I told no one what had happened at that evening service because I was not sure of what had happened, or how to explain it. It was not until after Adam died that I would reflect on that event and begin asking God questions, looking for meaning in it.

After Adam died I sought for the presence of God anywhere and everywhere I could in my life. Although I had done that in my life before, now seemed different. Now, I was on a quest. Now, I was looking for answers, meaning, and reasons.

That evening, at our little church on a Thanksgiving Eve, I truly believe that God had opened a window of Heaven and allowed me to hear a choir of heavenly angels singing along with our little church. It was awesome, beautiful and majestic. Most of all, it was comforting, reassuring to know God Himself, manifested His powerful presence at our little church service that night… with a miracle.

Looking back on the event, I'm not sure what the intent of this miracle was, except to say that maybe God was simply demonstrating that He *is* close, and He *is* real. Perhaps God, being all knowing, was opening my heart and mind to the presence and acceptance of miracles because I would soon need them to find peace with Him after Adam's death.

He knew I would be searching for answers to questions not yet asked. Adam's death would not come for nearly another year. Perhaps God was preparing the way for my heart to receive His miracle messages, His answers to my cries.

Three Monarch Butterflies

On August 8, 1997, the day of Adam's funeral, a couple of very close friends, Becky and Todd, witnessed three monarch butterflies circling above us as we sat next to Adam's casket at the gravesite. Becky is the daughter of our pastor at the time and Todd is her husband who is also a pilot of airplanes. He and Adam had a rich relationship. There were also dozens of friends and family that surrounded us, crowding in towards the place where we would lay our son's body to rest. With the pastor standing on one side of Adam's casket and us sitting on folding chairs on the other, the graveside service proceeded.

Becky and Todd had been at the tail end of the mile-long funeral procession from the church to the cemetery. The procession was nearly two miles long, as stated by one of the motorcycle escorts. Parking at the cemetery was full, forcing Becky and Todd to park across the street in the college parking lot. They quickly found their place among the crowd, on a slight rise of the small hill just behind us, as the pastor began his eulogy.

As we all listened to our pastor speak, Becky and Todd noticed that just above our heads, about four to six feet above us, there were three monarch butterflies, flying in a tight circle. They related to us later that the butterflies just stayed there, flying in a circle above our heads for the duration of the graveside service. They circled us until everyone left. They thought it was curious how these three monarch butterflies, with all those people present, would remain so close to only Linda and me.

We didn't think much about it, since it was the fall season with the southward migration of the monarch butterflies in full swing. Butterflies were everywhere, flitting from flower to flower as they made their way south by the thousands. At the time, we just didn't think much of it. We simply dismissed it as an observation without an explanation. There were simply too many other pressing things to think about at that time of our grief.

About a week later, Linda and I went to visit the grave of Adam's student, Jason, to pay our respects with flowers and a note of love. As we approached Jason's grave for the first time, we noticed that there were striking similarities with his headstone and Adam's. Both are polished ebony with white lettering, and most remarkable is that they both have a scene of an airplane and a sunset.

As we stood at Jason's grave, reflecting on the similarities of their gravestones, I noticed some movement just above our heads. I looked up and directly overhead I saw that there were three monarch butterflies flying in tight a circle, just above us. They remained there until we left. Later that evening I began to search for a meaning to this miracle through prayer and meditation. There had to be a connection, a reason it happened.

I began to break down the elements of the event to see what, if any, meaning there could be in it. There was a funeral, depicting the end of a human's life on earth... the circle of life. There were three butterflies. Not just any type of butterfly, but monarch butterflies... each time flying in a circle... over our heads... until the end... repeated, again at Jason's grave in a different cemetery. Coincidence? No, it was a miracle. It was a miracle message from God to comfort our hearts.

As I pondered what the message was, I reasoned that the circle represents God, eternal with no beginning and no ending. Next, the butterfly is symbolic of the Christian life, the transformation from our earthbound life to the eternal, heavenly life by being *born again*; shedding the old earthbound shell for one with wings to wander the heavens. And, lastly, that the monarch is considered the king of butterflies, representing Christians, that the Bible promises will one day rule and reign with Jesus.

The Bible says of Jesus that He is called "…King of Kings, and Lord of Lords…" Believers in Jesus Christ are promised to "…rule and reign…" as kings. Each time I see a butterfly I remember this event, and I stop and thank God for His Grace and the power of His love for me in Jesus Christ, who died that we can live forever … and be filled with Joy. Oh, another thing… Adam had a saying, *"Everything comes in threes."*

<div align="center">~~~~~~~~~~~~~~~~</div>

666 LTD

About two weeks after the funeral, I found that I was beginning to waiver in my faith. I felt I was losing it, literally. I could sense something deep in my spirit becoming dark, void of my relationship with God. I felt as if something was literally sucking the life out of my faith and that the very substance of my faith was being pulled out of me.

I could feel all the dark emotions of grief smothering my faith in the only One who could help me through my grief – God. Anger, frustration, fear, shame, doubt, anxiety, confusion, worry, isolation and the feeling of abandonment all came rushing in, like a tsunami wave swallowing my faith. Deeply frightened, I went to God in prayer...

"Dear Lord, please, I am so afraid. I have lost my son and the pain is unbearable. But Lord, now I am starting to lose my faith in You as well. I can't stand to lose my faith too. Please, help me. Please don't let me lose my faith in You. I can't bear it. Please, help me Lord."

I needed to go back to work that day, as I had already lost two weeks from work mourning the death of my dear son. It was noon as I headed in to the office. Approaching an intersection where I would be turning, I stopped at a red light.

As I approached I noticed the license plate of the car in the lane next to mine. It had one of those message frames secured around it, that it had something to do with aviation. Not paying full attention I moved over into the right turn lane, and after looking for traffic I began to make my turn. At

111

that same moment, the lights changed to green and the car to my left began to move through the intersection.

As I continued making my turn I heard, what I've come to believe, the Lord telling me to *"look at the license plate."* It was that same audible voice I had heard in my car weeks before. Startled, I glanced over my shoulder to look. I noticed a handsome young man (like Adam) driving the dark blue car with one of those license plate frames on it.

This license frame read, *"I love flying."* Adam drove a dark blue car years earlier and also had one of those aviation license frames on it. What an extraordinary similarity to Adam's car, and how deeply it reminded me of him. I remember thinking to myself, *"here is a young pilot, just like Adam."* I continued to drive on. Then the voice became louder and said to me…

"READ THE PLATE!"

I quickly looked back at the aviator's little blue car as he made his way through the intersection. As he drove away, I read the license plate. It read "666 LTD"! He drove off and I continued through my turn, feeling quite bewildered, wondering if I was losing my mind. But within just moments, God began to speak to my heart, as I reflected on what possible meaning there might be in that message on the plate. Then God came in loud and clear, and began speaking to my heart:

"666 is the mark of the beast – Satan, the devil. LTD is the abbreviation for the word limited. My message to you is this: The devil is limited! I AM your God, there is no other. I AM in control, and will never leave you nor forsake you. I have said it in my Word. You can trust in me, Mark."

Abruptly the car went silent. Once again and with a bit of fearful but confident reassurance, I could sense my faith-strength being restored. I was stirred within myself that something very significant had just occurred. I've come to believe that God sent me a miraculous message on the license plate of a young pilot, like my dear son Adam to restore my faith.

It struck me as ironic that God would communicate his power and love, in answered prayer that required the very faith I was so fearful of losing. I pondered these things in my heart throughout the day, faithfully listening for the voice of God to speak to my heart again.

~~~~~~~~~~~~~~~~~

The Lost Red Pen

I have been accustomed to carrying a red and a black felt tip pen in my personal appointment calendar for over twenty years. It just became a habit with me. The pens always sat side-by-side in the front flap of my appointment calendar like a couple of obedient soldiers ready for service. A miracle message was in the making, a very special message from God to help me in my struggle with my grief, sorrow and my shame. The message would come through an event involving one of my two little soldier pens that rested in my appointment calendar.

One Sunday, late in the evening, I found myself at the cemetery in prayer. That fact in itself was not significant since I spent a large amount of my time at Adam's grave, praying and reflecting on his life. I had a lot of conversations with both Adam and God on that grassy hillside of Adam's final resting place. But, I had now come to a place in my life that even though my faith had been restored by God's wondrous message on the license plate, I was now beginning to lose the essence of hope, one of the three things God's word says are "given" to us on the earth. "And now these three remain: faith, hope and love. But the greatest of these is love." 1 Cor. 13:13 NIV

Many weeks had passed since Adam's death and I remember deep feelings of confusion and fear surrounding the issue of my future as a husband, a father and a ministry leader.   I began feeling hopeless in my future!   Perhaps it was all just part of the grieving process.   I wasn't sure.   So, I went there that evening to ask God for His help, His guidance.   I needed something, I wasn't sure what it was, but I was experiencing a truly debilitating episode of grief, along with the guilt and shame of my behaviors up to and including the day Adam died.   I needed to ask God to restore and revitalize my hope.   I felt hopeless about my future and, quite honestly, my salvation, in light of all that had happened.   My prayer went something like this...

"Father, I come to You through Jesus Christ my Lord and Savior to ask You for some help in my life.   I am confused about where I am with You Lord, with life, with everything that's going on right now.   I miss my son so much.   I know he is with You Lord but it still hurts so very deeply to not have him here beside me.   You have restored my faith and I thank You very much, but Lord my hope is waning.   I have looked deeply at the sin in my life, my relationship with You, and now this calling on my life to begin a ministry.   I don't know what to do, Father. Please help me.   Your Word says, "...faith is the evidence of things <u>hoped</u> for."   I have faith, but I need the

evidence, tangible proof, something I can put my hands on that says You are still with me, that I am forgiven, that I matter. Father, I acknowledge that you are God, and I am not. I need You, Lord. I don't want to tell You how to do your job, but Lord... I think I need a miracle. Please, restore my hope. Thank You for listening, Father. I love You."

The next day, Monday, I went to the office as usual. There was a monthly meeting I needed to attend, so taking my appointment calendar and checking that my little felt tip pen soldiers were in their proper place, I trotted off to my meeting. Upon arriving, I grabbed a sweet roll and a cup of coffee and sat down, ready to take notes. When I opened the appointment calendar I discovered that I had lost the red pen. The meeting started.

When I returned to the office, around 10:00 am, I went to the company supply cabinet to replace the red felt tip pen I had lost. There on the shelves in our office supply room were rows of plastic bins containing the plethora of office supplies needed in our daily activities. Row upon row of bins containing paper clips, white out, folders, binders and of course, pens. I located the bins with the pens in them. There was the one with blue pens, one with black, even one with purple. Aha, there it was, the bin with all the red pens I could ever need.

Being somewhat fussy about what type of pen I used, I searched that bin for a felt-tip pen. I just could not find one felt tip pen. Every pen in that bin was a large, fat roller ball type. I must have checked over fifty pens before I felt a bit embarrassed for being so picky. I looked at the last one and sure enough it too was a roller ball. So, I just took it back to my office and placed it along side the thinner, black felt tip soldier that I had had for so long. Looking at them, I thought how different they looked side-by-side. Closing my appointment calendar, I went back to work.

About 3:15 that Monday afternoon, walking back to my cubicle from talking with one of my business associates, I felt an extremely strong compulsion to reach for my appointment calendar before sitting down. I vividly remember thinking *"Why am I doing this?"* and then looking inside to discover that both of my pens, the black and the red were still there, safely tucked away for future use. Again, I wondered to myself *"Why am I doing this?"* thinking that perhaps I had somehow forgotten something I was supposed to do or somewhere to go, something like that.

It was as if I couldn't let go of the appointment calendar, that something outside of me was causing me to look deeper. As I stood there, holding my appointment calendar on-end, looking into it from the top, I discovered that the red pen seemed to stand out for some reason. I pulled it from its place and discovered that it was not the fat roller ball I had placed there just a few hours earlier, but that it was in fact the very pen I had lost – it was the original red felt tip pen!

Now I was really confused! Again, I felt as if I was going insane. I turned to my business associate, Carol, who sat just across the aisle from me, and I asked her if anyone had been in my cubicle that day, if she had seen anyone touch my appointment calendar. She told me that she had been in her office the entire day and saw no one enter my office. She seemed deeply concerned and asked why I needed to know that. She said it looked like I had just seen a ghost. She assured me no one had gone into my office all day. I just sat down, completely bewildered. I didn't know what to think of it all.

Each day that week as I drove both to and from work (an average of one hour travel time each way in rush hour) I thought about the red pen. *"Could I be going crazy?!?"* *"Did I imagine it all?"* *"Did someone find the red pen and put it in my appointment calendar?"* By Friday I was beside myself with confusion and in fear that I was losing my mind. I replayed each detail of the event in my mind, over and over and over again. I held firm to the knowledge of what I knew to be factual… *"I DID NOT IMAGINE THIS!"*

Saturday came and I learned that I would be alone in the house for the morning since Linda would be out shopping. So, since I had the morning to myself, I decided to take it once again to the Lord for help, in prayer. I began asking God to help me uncover the truth about what had happened that previous Monday. As I prayed, God began to speak to me about what had happened, and even gave details in the miracle message.

He reminded me that the previous Sunday I had gone to Him asking for a miracle to restore me to Him, to give me hope. Now it was becoming clear that my God had answered my prayer – again! I realized, after some long prayerful meditation and humble request, that He had answered my prayer and provided me with a miracle, and that I was very thankful for it. But I didn't understand why it happened the way it did. I mean, why lose a red pen and restore it to me. Why not the black one, why not my wallet, why not the appointment calendar?

I asked Him what was significant about how He chose to answer me. I worked it out with the Lord for over three hours, alone, there in my house that Saturday morning, and I believe I was given many answers and messages within the miracle.

First, there was the miracle itself. My red felt tip pen was restored without any possible explanation. Second, there were specific messages I needed to hear from Him and this was just simply the way He chose to provide them to me. In my strong disobedience to God I had sinned against Him the day my son died. I desperately needed His forgiveness and ached in my soul for Him to restore me to Himself.

The red pen was chosen because it represented many things about restoration that pertained to my situation. God began revealing to me the symbolism of the message and each significant part in it.

A pen was chosen because it represents the instrument used in the written word. I was searching for restoration from God for all the wrong in my life, thus feeling a deep sense of hopelessness. He showed me that true restoration comes from God's written Word.

Ok, I got that one. He then showed me how the red pen represented the blood of Christ, which is needed to restore mankind to God. And even though I had replaced (restored) a different red pen to my appointment calendar it was God that restored the original pen, meaning that only He can truly restore us to Him, and only through the blood of Jesus Christ! I had already received that gift of salvation from God when I was only twelve years of age, but through the deafening trials of life as an adult, and now the death of my son, I seemed to have lost sight of it.

Then He showed me that the black pen represented the sin in my life, which will always be with me in this temporal, earthly existence, symbolized by the black pen remaining in my appointment calendar, my life-book. The appointment calendar itself was chosen to represent, symbolically, my life with all my duties, appointments and schedules. It represented the book of my life (to some extent).

God then revealed the importance of the timing of the event itself. His miracle-message happened on a Monday, at about 3:15 pm, the same day of the week and time of day that Adam had died. Certainly, that would not be significant to anyone but me.

I finally felt forgiven and, most importantly, *hopeful* in that I could be restored to Him and experience His grace and love. I needed His loving forgiveness so very much in order to look into my future, however long it might be.

Life is still very hard, harder in many ways than before Adam died. But having the assurance of forgiveness and restoration is paramount in the life of a Christian, especially one who found himself in the boiling pot of deception and hypocrisy as I did. Yes, life has presented more difficult challenges since then, but the hope remains alive and strong. And, the miracle messages continue to come my way.

~~~~~~~~~~~~~~~~

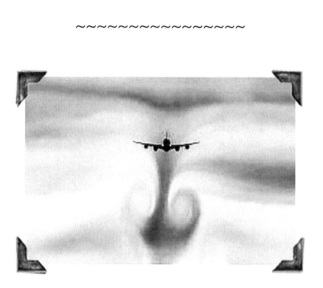

A Message Written In The Sky

Adam's favorite airplane was the Boeing 747. He actually flew one in a flight simulator at NATCO, the former Northwest Airlines training facility in Minneapolis. Ever since Adam was a child he had always loved all the different types of aircraft, especially airplanes. When Adam became a pilot and flight instructor he learned to identify many different aircraft just by listening to their engines. We tried to stump him often but to no avail. He really knew his stuff! Over time, he taught us to identify certain distinctive sounds as belonging to specific aircraft and soon we too were identifying airplanes just by hearing them (although not nearly as accurate as Adam).

About a month had gone by since Adam's death when I found myself back in the normal grind of duties around the house. Loving friends and family had done many things for us, but now I needed to give the lawn and gardens my own personal attention. I found a great deal of pleasure in working in my yard.

My lawn was thick and green, and my gardens were varied in size and style. From vegetables to perennials, butterfly to humming bird gardens, I usually took great care of it all... usually, but now the grass had grown high and weeds were beginning to creep into the gardens. It all needed serious remedial care, so I went to work on it that Saturday morning with my mind still fixed on Adam.

I was out in the back yard mowing the grass alongside the swimming pool, always careful to blow the grass away from the water, so as to not plug up the filters. Working my way around the perennial garden and the pond, I carefully sculpted the lawn with the mower. As focused as I was on my task at hand, I couldn't stop thinking about Adam.

I wanted him to come home, to be back with us and realize all the dreams we had for his life. I wanted him to come running around the corner and hit the pool with a huge splash, attempting to soak me while I mowed the lawn, something he did with regularity. I wanted him to drive up and ask if there was anything he could do to help me. I wanted him back. Period.

I agonized over the lack of knowing why he had to die. Even more, as a pilot and student of his, I was totally confused and dumbfounded as to how the accident itself could possibly have happened at all. Adam was such an incredibly gifted pilot. I felt like I was inside out; I desperately needed, wanted to talk to him. I wanted answers to so many penetrating questions. I continued to mow the grass, with Adam on my mind.

Over the annoying drone of the lawn mower, I could hear the distinct thunderous roar of a 747 approaching from the southeast. I shut the mower off and looked up only to see trees obstructing my view. So, I ran around the house to an area that offered a greater viewing of the sky. It was an overcast, cloudy day. The clouds were low, like in late fall when the air is cool and the sky drips tiny drops of rain that quench the earth just before the cold blast of winter sets in. Being a pilot myself I gauged the cloud base to be about eight to ten thousand feet. The 747 sounded like it was much lower than usual. I looked again across the dark gray afternoon sky. The sound of those four Pratt-Whitney engines was deafening. It sounded as if the 747 would pass just feet above my head.

The clouds, thick and gray, looked like a huge soft blanket that stretched from horizon to horizon, similar to a flat farm field covered with deep dirty snow. The engines roared and rumbled, loud enough to shake the ground under my feet. Massive, awesome and powerful were those four Pratt-Whitney engines, each with over 63,000 pounds of thrust.

The airplane was slowly plowing its way through the sky. I could not see it. I could only hear it, feel it shaking the ground I stood on. It seemed as if it were on top of me, it was so close. But, the only evidence that the huge craft had even been there at all was the deafening sound and the snowplowed look that the wingtip vortices had produced in that gray celestial blanket.

From horizon to horizon I could only see where the plane had been, not where it was. But it was clearly evident in the trail left in the sky that

Adam's favorite airplane; the Boeing 747 had just passed by. Then I heard his voice in my mind…

"Dad, stop looking for me. I'm in a place that you can't see. Just like you can hear the engines of the 747 you can hear my voice. But you can't see the airplane. Nor can you see me. But Dad, look where the plane has been. It has left a trail in the sky for you to know it was there. Focus on the trail of my life, dad. Tell them of my life. Tell them of my death. I'll see you soon."

He seemed so close, yet so far from sight. I called his name, but there was no answer. I called it again, louder. Still, there was nothing but the fading sound of Adam's favorite airplane disappearing into the cloudy afternoon sky. I just stood there, wanting him back. I didn't know what to think of it all.

I know that once a person dies he or she does not come back, it is what I've always been taught. Although, there are a few accounts in the Bible of the return of people who have passed into heaven; for example when Peter, James and John saw Moses and Elijah with Jesus on the Mount of Transfiguration. I've always been told that individuals don't come back from the other side. I've always believed it.

Now, with Adam speaking to me in this way, I wondered again if I was going insane. I told no one about it for months. But I could not let go of the sense of urgency that seemed to be in his voice that day. As months passed, I began to learn why.

I know that God's timing is always perfect, or else He is less than who He claims to be. With that in mind, I bend myself to trust in the perfection of His timing in all things... even Adam's death.

Please don't misunderstand. I hate that Adam died. I hate that I can't be with him, to watch him grow old, to hold his children on my lap, or share my golden years with him. I hate that his bride became a widow in three months, barely getting to know her handsome husband and *flyboy*. I hate that his mom's heart was broken into so many pieces that not even time could put them all together again. I hate that his sister Katrina never knew the pleasure of his children playing with her own. I hate death, all it brings, all it represents, and all that it does to us. But... I do trust in God, and in His timing.

Perhaps the message to me that day was both instructional and prophetic. It was instructional in the sense that Adam's voice guided me toward a goal, a purpose that would fulfill some need in the distant future. It was prophetic in the sense that I too would plow through the fog of grief, rumbling with noisy effort to make my way through the "clouds" of my life. But I would need more to complete my journey, my calling, of Adam's instructions. I would need to learn much, much more. And, so the miracles continued.

~~~~~~~~~~~~~~~~

Adam's Onyx Ring

Adam graduated from White Bear Lake High School in 1992. He received many gifts commemorating that glorious achievement. His favorite was a gold ring with a polished onyx stone set on the face. It was very special to him. It came from his grandma and grandpa Langton. The day Adam died he was not wearing his graduation ring, however he was wearing his wedding ring. In fact, his wedding ring was the only possession recovered from the accident. The fire that killed him and his student was so intense that even parts of the metal shell of the airplane had melted.

Nothing of Adam's was left except his wedding ring. I believe that was a miracle in itself. So did the folks at the mortuary that had received Adam's body and all his belongings from the Ramsey County Coroner's office. They couldn't understand how his wedding ring could possibly have sustained absolutely no damage from the intense fire that claimed his life. Linda now wears Adam's wedding ring on her hand, thanks to the generosity of his widow, Karin. But the other ring, the one Adam had received at graduation from his grandparents, was lost. Karin remembered seeing it on the bathroom counter the morning before his death. She told us that Adam would set it there when not wearing it. She remembers seeing it that fateful morning. That was the last time she saw the ring.

Not long after the funeral, we were going through all of Adam's baby boxes that were kept in our basement storage for posterity. We desperately needed to reconnect with Adam by any means possible. His personal "baby" items had been stored in our basement high on a shelf for many years. We went through all his memory boxes with the attention to every detail, like CSI agents processing evidence at a crime scene.

Each item pulled from a box brought a flood of laughter and tears and deep sobs as we recalled the intimate details of his precious life through the memories associated with it. It took hours to empty one box. We were completely spent in our emotions and wilted by crying so many tears that day. So many memories, so many tears.

I don't recall how many boxes we actually went through that day, but I do remember the very last one. It had been stored in our basement on a high shelf, in the back of other boxes of Adam's personal history, things we had stored at our home instead of sending along with Adam to his new one. We went through that last box even slower than the others, lingering on each item that was removed and cataloged them in our hearts as memories surged from times long past. These, his baby items, brought even more crushing delight and sorrow as we held each one with care.

As the final item was removed, looked at and reflected upon, bringing yet another surge of deep emotional pain and pleasure all at once, Linda noticed that there was something still in the box. She just sat there, staring into the large box for a long time, as if trying to solve a complex puzzle.

Quizzically, she looked up at me and then she simply reached into the box and pulled out Adam's graduation ring, with its polished ebony face and glowing golden band. She looked at me, shocked and puzzled. *"It's Adam's ring!"* she exclaimed. I didn't think it should be significant and must have said something to that effect.

Then she looked at me, deeply and with an expression that told me this was an enormously significant event. I asked her if perhaps Karin had placed the ring in the box and just forgot about it. Her reply made me fall back. She told me that the box was filled with baby items, kept in our house and had not been given to Adam when he and Karin got married. It had been sealed with shipping tape, and stored on the top shelf in the back of our storage area. There was NO WAY Adam's ring should be, or could be in THAT particular box! But there it was! We agreed that we had witnessed a miracle of God that day.

Miracles are awesome events. Sometimes they are bewildering, sometimes downright frightening. Always, we seek to try to understand the meaning behind such divinely inspired events. Often, the answers can come with deeply profound meaning, are intensely satisfying and provocative. However, sometimes they can delightfully simple.

I believe this particular miracle was a simple message of God's promise to restore to those who love Him. The ring is a symbol of eternity.

The stone represents our temporal life, here on Earth. The polished stone depicts the character of one who has done well, left a legacy of integrity, hard work and abiding purpose in his life. That well defines the life of our son. We got his ring back. It allowed us to get a part of *him* back that day. A precious part of his life that we thought was lost forever.

We will receive him to our arms again one day, and with joy unspeakable and we will rejoice and thank God for his beautiful life, for all of eternity.

~~~~~~~~~~~~~~~~

A Miraculous Message On The Computer

After hearing Adam's voice that day in that back yard, when the 747 roared by, I decided to build a web site in his memory, telling the story as he instructed. It was a simple site, not featuring much in the way of "high tech" wizardry that is so often evident in today's flashy web sites. Ours was just a simple, plain site with an important, life-changing story to tell.

As I learned (from scratch) how to build a web site, where to have it hosted and such, I decided to include a guest book. So, now we had a memorial web site complete with a guest book for our visitors to sign in and give us feedback, stories about Adam that would warm our hearts. Through the guest book page folks could send us messages of love and hope and encouragement. And many did.

Over time we received many heartfelt responses to our web page. This brought us a lot of encouragement and made us feel like we had accomplished a really good thing, especially when someone would write and tell us that as a result of reading the story of Adam's life and death on the web they accepted Jesus Christ as their Savior. Praise the Lord! But still, it was a *memorial* web site and as time went on, even in the midst of the wonderful stories about Adam, we continued to feel the clenching hands of grief and loss tighten around our hope and peace. One such time was just before Linda's birthday in June of 1998.

Holidays, anniversaries and birthdays, any day of significance brought us deep feelings of anxiety. They still do, although not nearly as intense and debilitating as they did in the first few years after Adam's death. Adam loved holidays, and always loved a good celebration. And his mom's birthday was a very special one to him, and we would soon discover yet another miracle of God, in the form of a very special message (from Adam) on her birthday.

One day, around the time of Linda's birthday, we noticed an unusual smudge on the guest book page of Adam's memorial web site. When I printed the page the smudge did not appear, however each time we went to the guest book page the smudge appeared again.

By this time I had immersed myself in HTML and web building, at least enough to know where to look for the source of the problem. Finding nothing, I enlisted the aide of Chad, Katrina's husband, since he is even more computer savvy and perhaps could help find the problem leading to the smudge on the screen. However, he could not explain it either. Everyone who looked into the matter was perplexed. "THAT should NOT be there!" they would emphatically announce, or "I can't figure that one out."

The smudge began to grow over the next few days, and soon would later show up in a printed version of the screen we were seeing. However, there was no definition to the screen abnormality and everyone dismissed it as a glitch of the computer or something like that. Then, one day while reading some additions to the guest book, I noticed that the smudge mark had grown again, this time it seemed to take on a shape. But, I needed a magnifying glass to see it. As I moved closer to the screen, focusing the huge eyeglass before me, the image of a heart came into view.

I printed it again. However, nothing but the same smudge image appeared on the paper. I called Linda in to see it and we were both awestruck with it, not realizing any significance with it at all... yet. I quickly launched an official investigation into the matter of the mysterious screen smudge, now forming a heart, appearing on our guest book page. I enlisted the aide of experts in web building, even tried those who hosted the site, all to no avail. No one could figure the thing out. Then I had an idea. "I wonder if anyone else can see it on their computers as well?"

When I went to work the next morning the first thing I did was launch Adam's web site, going directly to the guest book. No smudge, no heart! Nothing! I asked others in the office to do the same, each time yielding the same results. I wondered if it was a Macintosh vs. DOS machine issue, so when I got home that evening I sent out an email to everyone I knew asking for them to go onto the guest book page and report back what they saw at the top of the page, in the middle, just under the heading.

No one saw the smudge or a heart either for that matter. No one saw *anything*! It appeared that the smudge-turned-heart only appeared on *our* Macintosh computer. We were (and are still) convinced that it was a message to Linda on her birthday from her Adam. The message? *"I love you, Mom, Happy Birthday."*

Not long after this whirlwind event, we began experiencing some difficulty with our computer and the connection we had with our internet provider. We soon discovered that we could find another provider, upgrade the computer (an expensive venture), or buy another more compatible computer for our use. Since we expanded our ministry work with our memorial scholarship fund and "Love Basket" ministry,[1] we decided to donate our Macintosh to a family whose son had recently died, and they had to use their pastor's computer at the church to get email. We were happy to donate it to them, later meeting them over dinner. They were so grateful and we were happy to help.

We bought our new computer, which was much faster and had a lot more memory, all the "stuff" we needed to grow into. Sadly, when we launched onto the guest book we discovered the heart was gone. Thinking that it most certainly was the Macintosh that produced that mysterious smudge heart, we contacted the family in South Dakota that we had donated the computer to, asking them to confirm if the smudge heart was still there. They wrote back the next day asking, "What heart? What smudge? We can see nothing on the screen that you are talking about." It was clear that the smudge heart was now gone… forever. It then became clear to us that the Love of our Heavenly

---

[1] LNF Ministries, established in 1997, is our non-profit organization, which oversees *The Adam M. Triplett Memorial Scholarship Funds*, and the *Love Basket Ministry*. Our scholarship funds serve to financially support both high school music students and college-bound students in learning disciplines that exemplified Adam Triplett's life; aviation, music and Christian ministry. Our *Love Baskets Ministry* is a grief-support ministry, which offers grief support primarily to parents grieving the death of a child. Visit www.lnf.org.

Father was made evident in a simple message, from Adam, on a computer screen for a short time, on Linda's birthday. The message...

"I love you, Mom."

~~~~~~~~~~~~~~~~~

Another 747 Trail in the Sky

During the summer of 1998, almost a year following Adam's death, I was again out in the yard cutting the grass. This time I was in my front yard. It was a hot, muggy summer day and there was a thin haze layer in the atmosphere above. As I worked my way across the lawn, back-and-forth, I noticed a strange thing happening overhead. Like the 747 that had passed so low in that grey sky the previous fall, this too was a 747 flying overhead, only this time it was very high in the sky. The aircraft was very high in the atmosphere, probably at an altitude of twenty five to thirty thousand feet, flying on a Victor airway to some destination far away. At first the only thing I was really interested in was the fact that it was another of Adam's favorite aircraft, the huge 747. I turned the mower off and began to watch the aircraft make its way from west to east, as it crawled high above the earth. There was a haze layer above me that made it difficult, but not impossible, to see the airplane. The telltale sign of four vapor trails behind the aircraft confirmed that it was the mighty Boeing 747.

I didn't notice it at first, but as I continued to watch the aircraft flying overhead I noticed it seemed to be following a path in the sky, a path created by it's own vapor trail. The position of the aircraft, being higher than the haze layer below caused a shadow to be produced by the sun above the plane. As it flew from west to east the sunlight cast a shadow down onto the haze layer beneath and ahead of the aircraft.

The strange thing was that the 747 looked as if it was traveling along a predetermined route, a "path" in the sky. It never wavered from left to right, but stayed true to the path ahead of it. The angle of the sun was behind the 747, casting a shadow of the aircraft AND the vapor trail it was producing onto the haze layer beneath it and ahead of the actual aircraft.

The shadow on the haze layer looked like a road, or a path in the sky ahead of where the 747 was flying. It flew absolutely along that path, never moving away from it. Evidently, the angle of the sun to the airplane and its route of flight had to be in perfect alignment for this phenomenon to occur.

This time I did not hear any voice giving me instruction or direction, just children playing across the street and neighbors laughing at stories being told, and cars occasionally driving by. It was a normal Saturday afternoon in the hot summer. As I watched, I began to think about the rare event and I attempted to draw some meaning from it, as I had done so many times before when strange or rare events occurred.

By this time I was now quite experienced at seeing, listening and experiencing the miraculous hand of God. I thought there must be some significance in it, even though I heard no voice from Adam or from God at that time.

As I thought about the event and tried to apply it to the calling from the year before I came to the conclusion that there indeed was a message, albeit a silent one, that I needed to press on in the writing of this book, Adam's story… God's never failing love. I began to think of myself as the 747, Adam's favorite airplane, making my way through this life guided by the presence of God with the light of His word casting its shadow of my life ahead of me, helping me to keep true to the path chosen by Him for me.

I thought of how clear the sky was above the airplane, like the clarity of God's wisdom and love is so high above me. I thought too of how the aircraft, even with four very powerful engines, must plow its way to its destination. It too must press on using all its energy to stay aloft keeping its cargo of precious souls safe. I thought of the haze layer beneath the aircraft and how it seemed to represent the uncertainty and confused nature of life on earth.

I thought of how difficult it was to see through that layer, but could be guided through it because of the light that shone from above.

Reflecting on that event it is clear to me that God's miracles are often overlooked and dismissed as casual, "normal" occurrences of nature. Guided by this sense of reason and an abiding faith that the God of the universe communicates with me, with all of us, on a regular basis I too, like that 747 plowing its way to a predetermined destination, must press on with the calling of God on my life.

I started the mower, and over the drone of the motor mixed with the laughter of children and neighbors telling stories and cars occasionally driving by, I pondered these things in my heart, and gave thanks.

~~~~~~~~~~~~~~~~

Do Not Be Discouraged   Joshua 1:9

When I wrote about this particular miracle it had been nearly three and one-half years since Adam died. January 30, 2001 was a particularly difficult day for me. So much effort had been poured into our ministry work with very little to show for it.

I had begun to feel like a failure to God, to the ministry work, to Adam. I would say that January 30, 2001 was an all-time low as far as personal discouragement is concerned. So, I prayed.

"Father, I am feeling very discouraged lately. The work we have done for the ministry seems to have flattened out, turned stale. I feel as if I have failed You, Lord. I have begun thinking that I have made it up myself, for myself, and that it does not have Your blessing. Perhaps I should

just go back to work and live my life quietly until You call me home. I could really use a bit of encouragement Lord. I want so very much to serve You in this ministry. I'm trying to follow Your calling and I think I am on track, and then it feels as if the bottom starts to fall out again. I feel under attack! Lord, please send me even a small bit of encouragement. Thank you Father, I love You."

The following day, January 31, 2001, I received an email message from a very popular Christian recording artist named Phil Driscoll. Phil was one of Adam's favorite trumpet players. In fact, Phil was probably just as *instrumental (pun intended)* in Adam's faith walk as he was in his musical successes.

More to the point, in large part due to Christian artists like Phil Driscoll, Adam earned the privilege to play his trumpet at Orchestra Hall in Minneapolis in his senior year of high school, as a featured artist at the Minnesota All-State Jazz Ensemble.

Now, I realize that Phil's message that day went out to thousands of his fans, but what I find miraculous in it are these <u>three</u> things:

1. <u>The Timing</u> Answered prayer in one day! God's timing is always perfect. *(Romans 5:1-11)*

2. <u>The Message</u> Specific detailed answers to my prayer. He encouraged me by strengthening my hope!
   (1 Thessalonians 5:11)
3. <u>The Messenger</u> Phil was one of Adam's heroes. God's choices are gracious! *(1 Thessalonians 5:11)*

On the following page is the miraculous answer to my prayer directed by God, through my brother in Christ, Phil Driscoll.

You can decide for yourself if this is a miracle or just a coincidence!

* * *

Phil Driscoll Ministries E-Letter:

Dear Mark and Linda:

The technology that we have today at our fingertips is almost beyond words. To think that I can sit down and communicate to you from my heart and get it to you without having to wait days excites me. That means if God gives me something to share to strengthen you, I can get it to you faster and you can be encouraged quicker than ever before.

Whenever the New Year rolls around, I always take that time to reflect, to plan, and to regroup in my own personal life and ministry. I am convinced that one of the most successful tactics of darkness is to bring circumstances into our life to discourage us, to cause us to lose hope and back away from our God given dreams.

I wanted to take this moment to simply encourage you to not give up on your dream. Proverbs 29: 18 says, "Where there is no vision, the people perish." You could say where there is no 'God given dream', the people can't win; but whenever God's vision for your life stays alive on the inside of you, you can't die and you can't lose! No matter where the devil may be attacking you --- on your job, your family, your health, or anywhere else, he has never come up with any challenge that faith in God can't fix. But you will have to use your faith!

The God given joy on the inside of you is not just there for looks or to make you more attractive, it is an igniter of faith. It is not dependent on your circumstances; it is solely dependent on your decision to walk in victory by faith, to act like God's word is true, and to make the sounds of praise (of victory) like you had already won!

There is something that happens on the inside of you when you hear yourself shout, let alone what it does to your enemy and how it affects your battle. The victory sound, born on the inside of you when you received Jesus as Lord, is an important key to your winning. Remember,

'as the sound goes in your world... so goes your world'.
Keep that victory sound continually in your ears and in
your atmosphere and you will see victory with your eyes.
Your friend and brother,
Phil Driscoll

After meditating on the email from Phil Driscoll, as instructed in God's Word in Joshua 1, I am humbled by the reminder of being courageous and not being afraid.

Being encouraged is one thing, it was certainly a miracle in itself, but when I think of the way God has woven His love into the message, and the messenger using Adam's most favorite Bible verse, it leaves me astounded.

~~~~~~~~~~~~~~~~

What a Wonderful World

There's a wonderful, elegant restaurant just south of Minneapolis along hwy 13 in Mendota Heights called Jensen's Supper Club. It's quaint, quiet, elegant and rich with atmosphere. The food is superb with staff who are always inviting and warm. Approximately ten years after Adam's death, Linda and I were meeting a couple there for dinner at Jensen's, Marjorie and Daryl Sanborn. They had sent us a letter telling us of the death of their son, Jeremy.

We had never met the Sanborns, but we would find out soon enough that our sons had some incredibly amazing things in common. Over dinner they shared their own personal story about the death of their son. Jeremy died in an airplane accident in Indiana on September 12, 1997, just five weeks after Adam. The Sanborns' account of their

146

son's death would turn our worlds on end. We would come to learn that Jeremy was killed on September 12, 1997 in a plane crash while instructing students in Purdue University's flight program.

There were striking similarities with both boys. Both were committed Christians, with a strong desire to serve the Lord Jesus in aviation, played trumpet in High School, became flight instructors and died while conducting routine training flights in the exact type and model of aircraft (Beech BE76 Duchess), Adam at age 23 and Jeremy at age 24. The two boys even looked a bit alike.

The Sanborns had contacted us almost 10 years after the death of their son. They had read about our Love Basket ministry through an article in the local Christian Newspaper *The Minnesota Christian Chronicle*. Marjorie stated she kept it on her desk since 2003 and was triggered to find it after we had sent a Love Basket to acquaintances of the family.

Jeremy was with two students, practicing take-off and landings by doing "touch-and-goes" on a beautiful, cloudless Indiana day. They were barely into an ascent when the nose went down and they crashed before the end of the runway. No cause was ever found. All three aboard the aircraft were killed instantly. The plane burst into flames on impact.

Tears flowed at the table that night, the Sanborns telling us their story as if for the first time, with an intensity and raw nature that produced huge sobs around the table. We shared our own experiences with them, telling of some of the miraculous ways God was attempting to heal our hearts.

I remember quite vividly how at the end of our dinner, as we were leaving for the night, I became overwhelmed with compassion for this wonderful couple and offered any comfort and encouragement I could to soften the pain in their hearts. As we left the restaurant it began to rain. It was a downpour, actually. Oddly, Linda told me to wait with Marjorie while she went to get the car, something that was normally reserved as my duties.

Linda and Daryl went to get their respective vehicles, and I continued to share with Marjorie and encourage her of God's presence. I was interrupted by the mild sound of a song being sung overhead, in the speakers that were nestled within the canopy of the restaurant's entrance.

I asked Marjorie to stop, to listen, and to hear the sound of the song being sung overhead. She recognized it immediately to be "What a Wonderful World" by Louis Armstrong. There it was, right in front of us, confirming all of what I had said about God's presence and miracles communicating with us messages of hope and healing.

There it was. Adam's favorite song! *What a Wonderful World.* She gasped and fell silent; the cars approached, breaking the solitude of the moment. We all embraced and promised to meet again, here at this wonderful place, each year. She looked back and lipped the words, "*thank you*" as they drove off into the night.

~~~~~~~~~~~~~~~~

The Banister And The Book

A few years after the death of Adam, Linda and I made the decision to move from our little three-bedroom home and into a townhouse. We were depleted of energy, straining daily to understand and cope with our heavy grief. We wanted to run away from our sorrows, to escape the pain and confusion. We ran. It followed.

Yes, we sold our little three-bedroom home with its abundance of storage, friendly neighborhood, all of our beautiful gardens and the swimming pool. We left behind a decade of work remodeling our little home, creating and tending to our many gardens, and most of all we left behind the rooms where our children lived and grew.

We needed a change, more space in our hearts and minds to cope with the enormity of our loss. We didn't realize it at the time, but relocating did not remove any the strain or the pain we were immersed in. It couldn't.

As we carried our possessions into our new townhome, a split-entry style with staircases both up and down from the front door, our grief followed. We also discovered that first day that the banister to the stairway leading up to the main level had slivers. Nasty slivers. *"Well, THAT will have to be fixed right away!"* I thought.

That was in 1999. I had been attempting to write this very book that you are reading, struggling in my heavy grief and pain, straining to put to words the experiences of my life at that time. I had been writing since shortly after Adam's death.

Now, after more than a decade of living in our townhome, we have come to re-address the issue of that banister. It was still producing nasty little slivers and was really getting on Linda's nerves. I guess after 10 years pulling little stinging shards of wood out of one's hand can make one a bit irritated.

Shortly after moving into our townhome, Linda and I began attending Lakewood Evangelical

Free Church, now called Rockpoint Church. Through the nurturing of this fine family of Christian people, we found a new place to worship the Lord and be reintroduced into the mainstream of life.

One day, while chatting with one of the congregation members about the needs of our small congregation, we discussed the possibilities of helping those who can't help themselves. Linda came upon the idea of having someone else fix our dangerous banister, since it seemed I was either not able or interested in doing the job.

Enter Bill Bartolic, the general-contractor. Bill and Linda talked about how our church could form a group to help others in our church and in the community with house projects that were too much for them. Linda mentioned our banister and Bill's eyes lit up.

"Let me take a look at it and maybe I can come up with something for you," Bill said with enthusiasm. Linda's eyes lit up. I went to the coffee bar.

A few weeks, later Bill showed up with pencil, pad and tools needed to find a solution to our banister problem. Much talk ensued, and after a full tray of cinnamon rolls were consumed, Bill's assessment was complete.

His ideas were grand. So grand that we had to dismiss them due to the high cost involved. We scrubbed the project and left the banister as is. Which, at this writing, still stands in our hall stairway waiting to inflict those stinging slivers to whoever dares slide their hand while navigating up or down.

But, from that first encounter between Bill and Linda "Servants On Call" was born, a helps ministry now in full swing at Rockpoint Church. Through Servants On Call, we have been blessed to help many people with physical difficulties or age restrictions in the care of their homes and property.

The process was developed that would offer anyone the opportunity to call the church office and request a representative from Servants On Call to contact them about a need, usually something minor, but outside the range or ability to complete.

Such was the call in 2010, when Dr. Lisanne D'Andrea-Winslow, who wrote the *Forward* to this book, made a request for help at her home in Bayport, MN. Suffering from the death of her husband John, Lisa had become overwhelmed with the burden of taking care of a two-story, four-bedroom home with a huge yard and many gardens.

She was alone in her work. It was too much work for one person, too much for one with a broken heart. The church office contacted Linda and me about Lisa's request. We called Lisa and made arrangements to conduct the initial triage assessment of her needs and find solutions to them. What we found was far more than broken door latches, pictures needing hanging and children's swing set repairs. We discovered a deeply wounded, broken heart; a broken life.

Lisa's life was a parallel to our own in many ways, struggling with the deep sorrow, pain and confusion that the death of a loved one brings to a heart. We were connected immediately by our grief stories. Lisa showed us a book of poetry about her grief journey after the death of her son Bennett that she had written ten years earlier and we were struck to tears at the intensity, clarity and raw emotions that poured out from her broken heart and onto the pages.

Linda began to tear up within the first few paragraphs she read. I mentioned to Lisa that I suspected her book would be added to our Love Baskets. I was correct. Linda confirmed my suspicion and had me read the book also. Within the first page I too was in tears. That book, *"New Beginnings"* is now in every Love Basket we send.

At this writing, Dr. D'Andrea-Winslow has written and published six books. When hearing that, Linda stated, "Mark is writing a book too." Lisa insisted I send her a copy of my very rough manuscript, nearly a decade old by then, and offered to help me with the writing of it. After reading my manuscript, Lisa graciously offered to not only mentor me along the way, but to edit and help publish my book, this book. A simple insignificant thing like an old banister with slivers brought us together.

Under the loving care and guidance of God, miraculously, Lisa helped me complete a calling on my life back in 1997 when I heard my son's voice say, *"Dad…tell the story of my life."* God's love never fails. Sometimes it may take years to witness His loving handiwork, but the evidence of His presence is everywhere. Truly… Love Never Fails.

Every story in this chapter tells of the faithfulness of God to a hurting heart needing healing. In the days, months and even years after the death of a loved one, the pain, confusion, doubt and fear reside within us as a new addition to our very being. God performed many miracles confirming His great love for us in the early days after Adam's death.

These events, as you have read, were very affirming to us, and provided comfort and healing. These miracles continue to this very day. They continue to come as we diligently seek God and look for the messages in the miracle-language that we can hear and understand. These messages are each a unique, specific miracle.

Miracle, the very word miracle conjures up ideas and visions of mystical and magical events, inexplicable and mysterious. When looking through the eyes of fear, uncertainty and doubt miracles simply may not appear to exist at all. However, when looking through the eyes of faith we can learn to listen and hear God speak to our own miracle-language, to help us unlock the mysteries that surround us each and every day.

~~~~~~~~~~~~~~~~

*"Miracles happen today, and it's because of Faith.
Please, believe in miracles."*

~ Adam Triplett
Excerpt from Adam's sermon on Love in 1995
Wildwood Church, Mahtomedi, MN

CHAPTER SIX

Meaning

Unlocking The Mystery

This book was started back in 1998, shortly after the death of my son Adam. I worked on it for two years, off and on, as I struggled through the most difficult time in my life – the death of my son.

During this time Linda and I began to build our ministry and the scholarship structure of LNF Ministries. We desired to build an organization that would provide comfort and healing to the suffering, support to those seeking to serve God, and a deeper understanding of grief to others that have not walked through this dark valley of death.

The work of writing this book was difficult and I struggled to make sense of what I was doing and why. I needed to make sense of it all, to bring reason and purpose back into my life. But normal life would have no part of helping me along. More

157

struggle and trauma would plague our lives to the point where I was forced to set the book aside.

Having retired in 2000, my goal was to put all my time and effort into my writing and building our ministry organization. Within just a few months of retirement the bottom fell out of our dreams and goals.

First was the 9-11 attack on the World Trade Center, followed by an auto accident with a drunk driver that severely injured Linda. Soon after that, Linda lost her job and my photography business began to fail. The US economy was beginning to collapse and trillions were being poured into the banking system while my 30-year pension evaporated before our eyes.

Again, I found myself crying out to God for help. Days turned into weeks… weeks into months… months into years. The book was put on the back burner of our lives as we scrambled to adjust and make ends meet, to keep our heads above water.

We prayed daily for God's intervention, hoping for a clear message of what to do next. Then in the spring of 2010, while delivering a sermon in church one Sunday morning my Pastor asked a seemingly simple question of the congregation. He simply asked us, *"What are you doing with your life?"*

It seemed rhetorical, and we all sat there expecting him to reveal his scripted answer.

We waited a very long time for him to give us the answer, but there was only silence... a long, sustained silence. After what seemed like an eternity, he asked the question again, and again until the room was thick with tension. People squirmed in their chairs as Pastor Roy made eye-to-eye contact, fearing he might call on them to produce the answer. He just waited, in the deafening silence.

It was there, in those long moments of tense introspection that I heard the voice of God once again tug at my heart and mind..."*I told you to write the book.*" I rebutted the thought in my mind that no one would want to read it, that it wasn't relevant to today's culture, that it had no purpose or meaning to it. But, all I kept hearing Him say was, "*I told you to write the book.*" Pastor Roy relieved the tension in the room with a general answer to his question of us.

As he continued his message I felt reprieved from the cross-examination in my mind. However, for weeks I struggled with the question, "*What are you doing with your life?*" And, I struggled even more with God's answer to my heart. I didn't have any clue what else to write. I had already given an account of Adam's death and my struggles up to and including those times. I had already told about all the mysterious miraculous events in the aftermath of that time. But now what? What should I say, Lord? My answer to those questions would not come for many months, while I struggled to find meaning in it all. I just kept coming up with, *so what?* Then, over dinner with relatives, my answer came.

We were having a wonderful time of reminiscing and regaling each other at dinner with telling humorous stories of our past when my Uncle Hilliard mentioned he was thinking of writing a book about his life. Linda and I immediately applauded (we really love our Uncle Hilliard). Amidst the applause and cheers, Linda said, *"Mark's writing a book too."* They all seemed very excited to hear about it and began drilling me with questions from all sides.

I told them generally what this book was about and explained that I was stuck on the ending and that I didn't know what the ending of the book should be about and that I struggled with a sense of relevance about it. That's when my sweet cousin Beth began directing questions at me… *"How long have you been writing it?"… "What's it all about?" "Tell me more…"*

Within 5 minutes I had exhaled the deepest sense of purpose, intent and meaning of this book, which I believe was part of God's intention all along – that is, to reveal Himself to a broken world, a world filled with sorrow and grief, a message of His love to a world with broken and wounded souls, souls needing a reminder that *His Love Never Fails*.

That's when the meaning of this book became clear to me. I finally had a meaningful end, something to give my readers an answer to the proverbial "So what does it all mean?"

Meaning. We all seek it, whether in the mundane or the profound in life. We need to know the meaning of things, why things happen the way they do or even why some things happen at all.

When things happen that we don't fully understand, we reason, "Everything has some meaning in life. But, what does THIS mean?" These are some of the oldest questions known to humankind. We all demand answers to perplexing questions. "Why am I alive?" "What purpose do I serve?" "What is the meaning of life?" The list goes on and on.

The death of a child will most certainly cause the suffering person to beg for meaning in it all. I did. I asked many questions of God. "Why did my son have to die?" "Was I responsible?" "Have you stopped loving me because of my sin?" "WHERE ARE YOU GOD?!?" There were many, many more.

We search for meaning in these deeply profound questions. We need to know. It's what fuels our drive to learn, to grow, to survive, to function in life, to bring reconciliation or closure or peace, something meaningful.

When events outside of our understanding or comprehension happen, we often seek meaningful answers from others with greater knowledge or authority. Linda and I did.

We fought to understand our grief journey and enlisted the help of our Psychologist, Dr. Marcus Bachmann, and for over two years we carved out meaning in all our sorrows and trials. Many questions simply did not have easy answers, but we did find many meaningful answers to our grief and suffering, meaning and understanding that we could use to temper the pain of our grief.

I went even further. I personally sought answers from Dr. Ravi Zacharias regarding deeply painful questions. Dr. Zacharias is the internationally renowned Christian Apologist, considered by many to be one of the finest minds in the world. Dr. Ravi graciously and skillfully brought clarity and understanding and healing to my confused mind, broken heart and wounded soul, in his book *Jesus Among Other Gods*. (W Publishing Group, 2000).

Answers. We all want them. We humans feel entitled, somehow, to know all the what, why, when, how and who of the things that affect our lives. We simply want to know. We seek meaning. We all do, and when one is dealing with the aftermath of a trauma or tragedy, particularly the death of a loved one, especially a child, we have many questions. Questions that need resolve to bring understanding and peace back into our lives.

After Adam died I sought many answers from God. I had many questions, questions that came from the depths of my grief, sorrow, and shame. God answered me...in miracles. In the chapter *Miracles* I've shared many of the miracle messages God gave me in response to my many questions of Him at the time.

Those miracle messages answered my questions and gave resolve. For me, miracles became the language of God. It expressed His resolve on my life and gave me understanding to the things that seemed to be unraveling my life at the time. Miracle messages... sometimes shared with others and sometimes within the intimacy of my own personal relationship with Him.

In the end, meaning came by way of the miracle messages God spoke to me, and I found peace and resolve and healing from them. Since Adam's death in 1997 much has happened to us.

When we read bedtime stories to our grandchildren, we often read, "...and they lived happily-ever-after."

The reality is that there is no happily-ever-after in this life. "Life goes on," as they say, with all its trials and triumphs.

Well, within just a few years of the death of our son, I had developed the habit of wearing headphones to bed while listening to our local Christian Radio Station, KTIS in the Twin Cities. (98.5 FM) The music throughout the night soothed my soul, bathed my mind with words and music of praise and worship, something my soul needed desperately.

On one specific occasion, I recall pondering the question of God throughout the day regarding the question, "What's next?" "What should I do now?" I attempted to resolve my life with service or something approved by God to continue on. I wanted an answer. I needed one. I felt lost, again.

That night I put on my headphones as usual and dialed in to KTIS to wash my mind with the sounds of worship and praise as I drifted off to sleep. Hours later, I was abruptly wakened, as if shaken by someone. I became aware that a song was just beginning on the radio that would prove to be the answer I was seeking from God regarding my questions of the day.

The song was "Press On," by the Christian artists Selah. I knew immediately that it was God's answer to my questions, although I didn't particularly like it. "Press on?!?" "Press on...to what?!?" Now, I didn't say every answer from God is totally clear or even pleasant. In fact, in most cases a great deal of thinking and meditating is necessary to sort it all out. But, in the end, when God gives answer to a question, and assuming you first hear it and second act on it, peace will come.

Press on. I guess that means I get myself up, dust myself off and start all over again, every day. "Press on, Mark." "Keep going, Mark." "Don't ever quit, Mark." I hear You, Lord. I had to find out how to press on and God provided the answer in the completion of this book, my calling and understanding... my grief journey.

In the end, I am left with this simple equation: In all things of life, whether pleasant or painful, there is always God. And God is Love. And Love Never Fails.

I have experienced this truth with deep revelation, first-hand in my own life and through the experience of the death of a child. My child... Adam. With this new call on my life I can now press on.

"Ask and it will be given to you; seek and you will find; knock and the door will be opened to you."

Matthew 7:7 (NIV)

CHAPTER SEVEN

FRIENDS

A Word From Adam's Mom

About Friends

It's a very strange thing that happens when your life is put into a crisis mode. I remember reading in a book that your friends change when you begin the grieving process. I also remember thinking that I couldn't imagine friends leaving anyone that was going through such a terrible thing. It's strange to me that I remember that so clearly. In those early days after Adam's death, grief books were so important to me. They almost became a counselor to me when I couldn't talk to anyone else.

I was very overwhelmed with the support from friends and family and even acquaintances of ours. The day of the accident we had to wait to get official word that Adam had actually been in the plane and had died. We already had known since early evening, but we waited hoping that we were wrong. Our home was filled with people. My family was of course the first to arrive. Mark had called one or two people and they began calling others. My daughter arrived and then Adam's wife with her parents. I can still remember my dad getting out of his car and running to me, crying and just holding me.

I remember my sister driving up and seeing me, Katrina and Mark and screaming "No, not Adam!" There were people arriving constantly from our church. It amazes me to this day that the most vivid memories I have of that day and the days that followed were of people's faces, faces of pure sorrow and pain. By the time the sheriff and county pastor came at 11:30pm that night to officially declare our son dead, our home was filled with loving friends.

The days that followed are mostly a blur. My family was at our home day and night. I don't remember much except for them having coffee with me and sitting on the deck. The people that visited were too many to count. There were lots of hugs and tears. Even after the funeral, the people just kept visiting and bringing us food. We finally asked our pastor to announce at church that we needed some time alone. We would put a sign on the door saying "please do not disturb" and close all of the shades.   Then when the visiting slowed down I wanted them to come back. One of my fears at that time was that people would forget and figure we were fine after a few weeks. When friends would ask what they could do for me, I always answered, "Please pray for us and don't forget about us."   I couldn't imagine ever being "fine" and just picking up and going on. So when the visits stopped, I missed them. And when someone would stop over, I would get agitated that they were intruding. This thing called grief is the most confusing thing that I think I will ever go through!

We had a get together with all of Adam's friends and asked them to share memories with us. We talked with our church and let them know how we were doing. People that we had never met, but had their child die called us or wrote.   These were the people that I felt connected to, although when they said I could call anytime, I didn't.   Just knowing that they were there if I decided to talk was so comforting. In the beginning I had no desire to talk with anyone except my friends. What I found was that the books were right on.

Sadly, this process of grief causes people, even close friends to distance themselves. For example, I had a very good friend. We always saw each other at least once a month and would talk for hours. We also talked on the phone regularly. When Adam died I saw her a couple of times. I figured she saw how many were at our home and stayed away to let us visit with them.

Later, we went to dinner once. I started crying and I can remember she looked a bit uncomfortable. Soon after, she moved out of state without giving any prior notice. After she moved, we talked on the phone a couple of times. I wrote to her a few times and she didn't write back. When I asked her what was wrong, she just sent a note saying "nothing".

She didn't acknowledge my birthday, or Adam's one-year anniversary of his death. She no longer talks to me at all. There are others that have just stopped calling. I asked another close friend of mine that is still my friend, why this happens.

She thought it could be that they just don't know what to say. Now, isn't that silly? Of course I want to talk about Adam, but I also want to talk about all the other stuff that we have always talked about. Besides, if they truly were my friends they would want to ask me about Adam and my memories of him and their memories too.

Mark and I have been really confused by all of this. The people that we expected to stick around and get us through this are the ones that are no longer in our lives.

One hard lesson that I have learned from this is I have had three friends that have had children die, and although I was not so involved with them at that time, I really did desert them. I wrote letters for a while and then life went on as usual for me. I now realize how important it is to receive a note from a friend letting them know you are thinking about them. It takes so little time and means so much.

Another difficult area for me was, Adam's friends. They stayed in contact with us through the first year. They called our first Christmas without Adam, came to his birthday party, and called on the first anniversary of his death. But, their lives went on. One of Adam's best friends called one day to tell me that he and his wife were expecting a baby. While talking to him, I was so excited with the news. We laughed and talked for a long while.

When I got off the phone I was suddenly so sad. Other friends bought houses, had babies and got married. While I didn't want them to stop living or live in grief, I felt that they had forgotten Adam. Well over a year after Adam's death, I realized that they still love and miss Adam.

Life goes on, even mine. What made me so sad was that they were experiencing what Adam would have experienced if he were still alive. I'm not able to see him realize his dreams. He would be working for an airline now, planning on buying a house, raising his family. He would be reaping the rewards for his hard work. I am not able to see him enjoy that, to share his joys as an adult. I have begun to seek friends now. I have made a new friend that just lost her son a few months ago. Up until a short time ago, I was not ready for this. Whoever was here already was enough. My short amount of energy did not allow this extra mental and physical work of making new friends.

When I heard of this woman, through a friend at work, it touched my heart. It has been so healing for me because I am able to tell her what I am going through too. When she writes and tells me of something that has happened I am able to share with her what I did to get through it.

So, let me say this to the one that is reading this and is going through the storm of grief. Love your friends, feel blessed that they are around when you need them. If some don't stay to see you through the storm, don't worry. God seems to put just the right people into your life when you need them. It could be someone new, or it could be a friend from long ago. Don't be afraid to be yourself, to let yourself grieve in front of them. If they are really meant to be in your life, they will stick around and help you.

To those that are reading this and know someone that is grieving, please remember him or her. Don't say that you will be with them through this and then abandon them. They need to lean on others. If you aren't strong enough to hold them, tell them so. It is so important to be honest and open. A grieving person does not have any extra energy to use up worrying about such things as why you stopped calling or what they did to make you go away.

I encourage everyone reading this book, to open your heart to understanding how deep and complicated grief is. Grief is different for each person. Don't judge the grief process for them or yourself. A dear friend and counselor told me early on in my grief journey "it is all okay."

As long as I didn't hurt myself or anyone else, it was all okay. If I wanted to skip Christmas, if I wanted to spend hours at Adam's grave, if I didn't want to get out of bed for a day, it was all okay. It was my grief and I needed to do what I did to get through it. Grief is a lifelong process that does not end with the one-year anniversary, or any anniversary.

It is a process that requires, faith, hope, patience, support and most of all the miracle of love.

"The most astonishing thing about miracles is that they happen."

G. K. Chesterton